Drive and Stroll in

Cheshire

Brian Conduit

COUNTRYSIDE BOOKS
NEWBURY BERKSHIRE

First published 2009
© Brian Conduit 2009

COUNTRYSIDE BOOKS
3 Catherine Road
Newbury, Berkshire

To view our complete range of books,
please visit us at
www.countrysidebooks.co.uk

ISBN 978 1 84674 131 9

The cover picture of
Alderley Edge
supplied by Bill Meadows

Photographs by the author
Maps by CJWT Solutions, St Helens

Designed by Peter Davies, Nautilus Design
Produced through MRM Associates Ltd., Reading
Typeset by CJWT Solutions, St Helens
Printed in Thailand

Contents

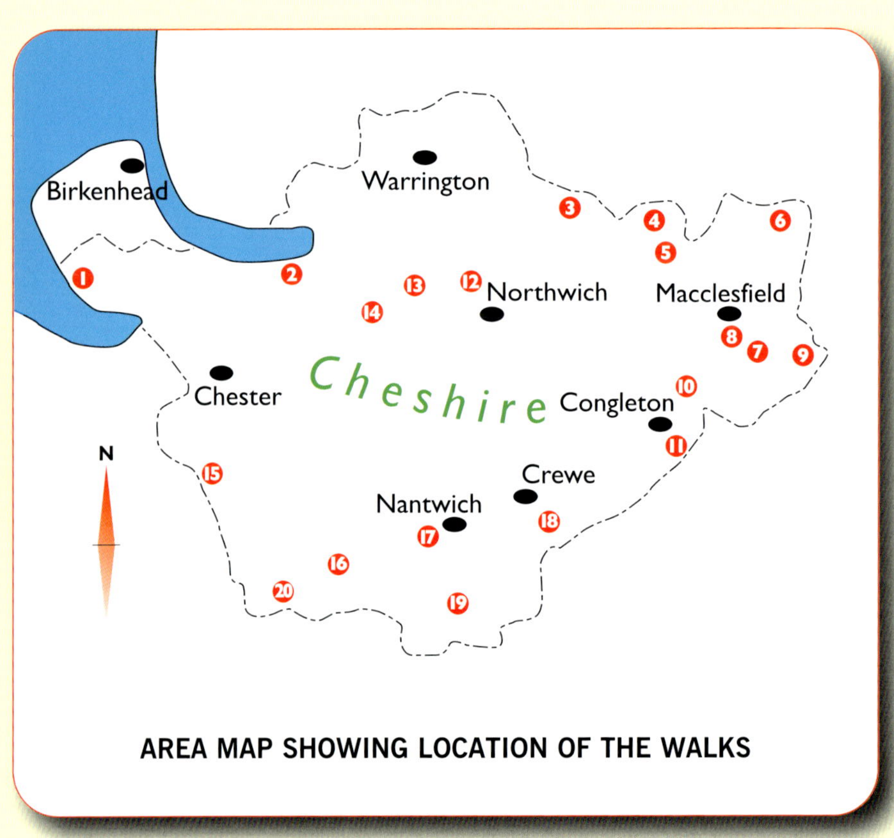

AREA MAP SHOWING LOCATION OF THE WALKS

Contents

PUBLISHER'S NOTE

We hope that you obtain considerable enjoyment from this book; great care has been taken in its preparation. Although at the time of publication all routes followed public rights of way or permitted paths, diversion orders can be made and permissions withdrawn.

We cannot, of course, be held responsible for such diversion orders and any inaccuracies in the text which result from these or any other changes to the routes nor any damage which might result from walkers trespassing on private property. We are anxious though that all details covering the walks are kept up-to-date and would therefore welcome information from readers which would be relevant to future editions.

The simple sketch maps that accompany the walks in this book are based on notes made by the author whilst checking out the routes on the ground. They are designed to show you how to reach the start, to point out the main features of the overall circuit and they contain a progression of numbers that relate to the paragraphs of the text.

However, for the benefit of a proper map, we do recommend that you purchase the relevant Ordnance Survey sheet covering your walk. The Ordnance Survey maps are widely available, especially through booksellers and local newsagents.

Many people from outside the county get a false impression of Cheshire as they rush through it, either while driving on the M6 or looking through the windows of a London to Glasgow express train. It appears to be a predominantly flat county, a county of rich pasturelands from where its famous dairy produce – especially Cheshire Cheese – comes.

In truth much of central Cheshire does consist of such country but this is only part of a much more diverse landscape. Look to the east and a line of hills can be seen on the horizon. This is the western edge of the Peak District, a landscape of high hills, steep narrow valleys and empty rolling moorland of millstone grit. Through this part of Cheshire winds one of its long-distance footpaths, the Gritstone Trail, as challenging a route as any in England.

On the horizon to the west another line of hills can be seen. This is a sandstone ridge, less rugged terrain and more wooded than the hills to the east but still steep in places. This is also traversed by a popular and rather less challenging long-distance footpath, the Sandstone Trail. Needless to say, from both ridges the views are extensive and magnificent.

Cheshire has some of the finest stately homes in the country, ranging from small black and white medieval and Tudor manor houses to great Georgian and Victorian palaces. Many of them are now owned by the National Trust and are surrounded by extensive parklands which provide countless opportunities for pleasant and relatively easy walks.

Cheshire is also criss-crossed by canals as, during the Industrial Revolution, the county occupied a strategic location between the industrial areas of the Midlands and the north-west. It also had industries of its own, notably textiles and chemicals in the north, and salt around Northwich. The canals were built across it to link these industrial areas with each other and with the river Mersey. Nowadays these once busy waterways provide attractive and tranquil corridors for walkers.

As well as varied and attractive landscapes, Cheshire contains some delightful old villages with picturesque black and white cottages – some thatched – several outstanding red sandstone churches and cosy pubs that not only dispense good food but also retain many traditional features such as stone floors, beams and open fires which only add to the pleasure of walking in the county. The 20 walks in this guide have been chosen to cover all parts of Cheshire, embrace all the different terrains and include many of the historic sites. I hope you enjoy them.

Brian Conduit

1 Parkgate and the Dee Estuary

The promenade at Parkgate

Distance 3½ miles **Terrain** Flat and easy walking, mainly along clear and well-signposted paths and tracks **Map** OS Explorer 266 Wirral & Chester (GR 273792)

How to get there

Parkgate is signposted from the A540 between Neston and Heswall. The Old Baths car park is just beyond the north end of the village, reached along the tarmac drive that passes in front of the Boat House pub. **Parking:** Old Baths free car park at Parkgate.

Introduction

The first part of the walk is through the village and former port of Parkgate that overlooks the marshes of the Dee estuary. You then turn away from the marsh and continue first along the Wirral Way (a disused railway line) and later along tracks above the estuary. Throughout the route you enjoy outstanding views across the Dee to the hills of North Wales but from the slightly elevated Wirral Way the views are particularly superb. In clear conditions, the walls of Flint Castle can be made out on the opposite shore. Finally a walk along the edge of the marsh brings you back to the start.

Refreshments

The Boat House pub is conveniently situated near the start of the walk. It also has a superb location on the edge of the marsh. If you have a window seat in the conservatory or choose to eat outside, when the weather is suitable, you can enjoy the grand views. As if that is not enough, the food is excellent as well. Cooked meals include fish, meat, steak and vegetarian dishes – plus Sunday roasts – and there is the usual wide range of sandwiches and lighter options. Telephone: 0151 3364187.

THE WALK

The car park occupies the site of the Old Baths, parts of which still survive. They are one of the few physical reminders of Parkgate's brief life as a seaside resort. The baths were built in 1923 by the headmaster of the local Mostyn School, initially for use by the pupils but later made available to the public for a fee. They were regularly washed by sea water but as the waters retreated and the marsh encroached, the baths were forced to close towards the end of the Second World War and they were later demolished.

Begin by walking back along the drive to the road by the **Boat House** and keep ahead along **The Parade** through **Parkgate**.

Parkgate was a thriving port in the 18th century, with a customs house, assembly rooms, inns, coffee houses and a theatre. Ferries from here sailed across the estuary to North Wales and there was a flourishing trade with Ireland. It is alleged that Handel put the finishing touches to the Messiah while staying here in the 1740s en route to Dublin.

Parkgate owed both its rise and decline to the vagaries of the river Dee. From Roman times up to the 15th century, Chester had been the principal port on the Dee but the silting up of the river caused its decline and led to the development of ports further downstream, to Neston and then later to Parkgate. But the silting up was a continuous process and was made worse by the digging of a new channel in the 1730s which favoured the Welsh side of the estuary. By the early

Looking towards Parkgate from the Old Baths

years of the 19th century Parkgate was in decline; an obvious sign of this was the transfer in the 1830s of the passenger services for Dublin to Liverpool. Parkgate enjoyed a brief heyday as a fashionable seaside resort but that was also ended by the relentless spread of the marsh and the further retreat of the river. Now, instead of developing into another Liverpool or Birkenhead, Parkgate is a pleasant backwater where the attractive black and white buildings and white-painted cottages that line The Parade overlook thick marsh.

At the end of **The Parade**, follow the road to the left (now **Station Road**) and where it bends right, turn left, at a Cycleway sign, onto a tree-lined track, here joining the **Wirral Way**.

The Wirral Way is a footpath and cycleway that extends for 12 miles along the western side of the Wirral Peninsula, following the course of a former railway. The railway opened in 1865 and originally ran between Hooton and Parkgate but was later extended northwards to West Kirby. It provided a link between Chester and Liverpool and transported both goods and passengers. The sharp decline of traffic after the Second World War led to its closure in 1962 but fortunately most of it remained untouched and undeveloped to allow its later conversion into the present attractive and well-used recreational amenity.

After left and right bends, the track continues in a straight line.

 ②

Just before crossing a bridge, bear left down steps, turn right under the bridge and walk along an enclosed track to a T-junction. Turn left along a broad track to a road, cross over and continue along the track opposite. Just beyond a house and farm buildings, where the track curves left, keep ahead through a gate and head downhill along the left edge of a field. Cross a footbridge at the bottom, keep ahead over the brow of a slight rise and on the far side of the field, veer left to a gate. Go through, continue along the right edge of a golf course and look out for where a yellow waymark directs you to turn right over a plank footbridge. Turn left and continue along a tree-lined path – still along the edge of the golf course – to a public footpath sign.

 ③

Turn left down three steps and follow a double line of blue posts across the course to reach a kissing gate. Go through, cross a track (the **Wirral Way** again), go through another kissing gate opposite and head across another part of the golf course to a footpath post by a bench. Turn left along a path which keeps along the edge of the marsh to return to the start.

PLACE OF INTEREST NEARBY

The fascinating model industrial community at **Port Sunlight**, the creation of Lord Leverhulme, is just off the A41 about 3 miles south of Birkenhead. After learning all about its origins and history at the Sunlight Vision museum, you can take a stroll around the village, visiting the Lady Lever Art Gallery and admiring the attractive houses built for the workforce, the communal buildings and the church. Telephone. (Sunlight Vision Museum) 0151 644 6466.

2 Above Frodsham and the Mersey Estuary

Distance 2½ miles, or 2 miles without the detour to Frodsham church and the Ring o' Bells pub **Terrain** Clear and well-signed field and woodland paths **Map** OS Explorer 267 Northwich & Delamere Forest (GR 519766)

How to get there

Frodsham is on the A56 between Warrington and Chester. From the town centre, turn up Church Street then turn right along Manley Road and head uphill. After about ½ mile, turn right into Simon Lane and Beacon Hill car park is on the right. **Parking:** Free car park on Beacon Hill.

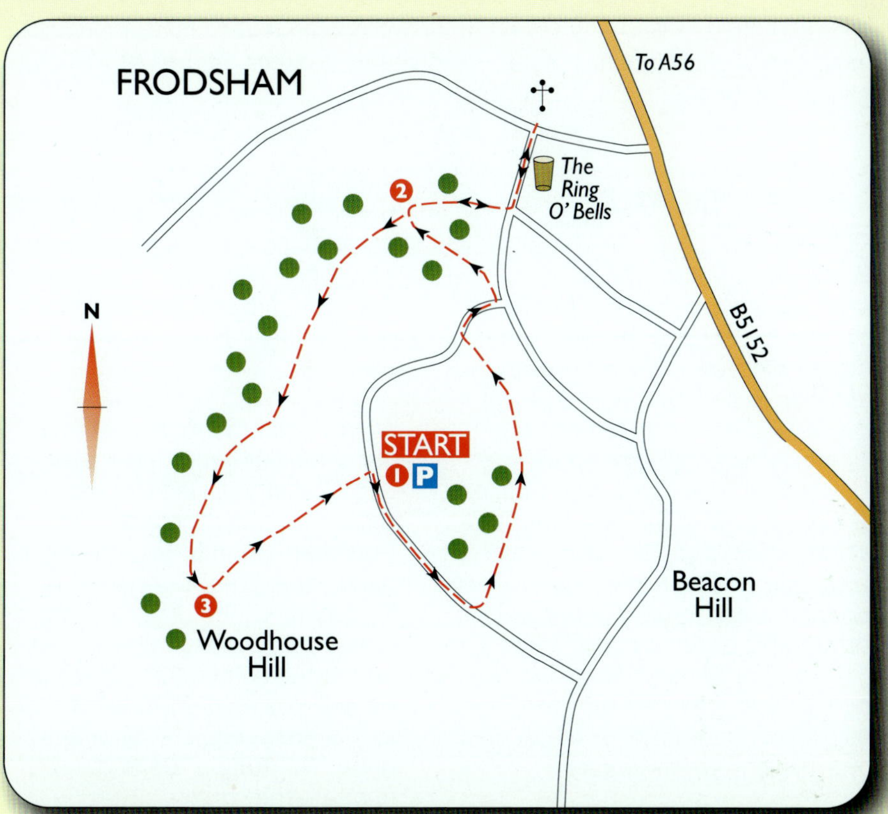

Introduction

One of the main advantages of this walk is that you start at the top of a hill and all the hard work has been done by the car. Also you lose very little height, unless you make the brief diversion to the Ring o' Bells pub by Frodsham church which only involves a modest descent and ascent. Although a short walk, it is full of interest and includes a medieval church, outstanding views across the Mersey estuary, delightful woodland and some spectacular rock formations.

Refreshments

There are pubs and cafés in the centre of Frodsham, while on the walk itself you pass three pubs, although two of these involve a brief detour from the main route. One of them is the **Ring o' Bells** opposite Frodsham church. This is an exceptionally cosy pub, full of atmosphere and with lots of small rooms and open fires. It serves pub food at its finest, with a wide choice of cooked meals and lighter lunches (soup, sandwiches, toasties, etc) all at moderate prices. Telephone: 01928 732068.

THE WALK

While driving along the M56 between Warrington and Chester, the eye is drawn to two prominent hills to the south which fall away abruptly to the flat land bordering the heavily industrialised Mersey estuary. These hills are above Helsby and Frodsham, with Beacon Hill being part of the one that rises above Frodsham. The Sandstone Trail, one of Cheshire's long-distance trails, begins in the town centre and climbs up to the war memorial at Mersey View, passed on the walk. The trail runs for 34 miles from here to Whitchurch, just over the Shropshire border.

Turn left out of the car park along the lane and at a footpath post indicating that you are joining both the **Delamere Way** and **North Cheshire Way**, turn left along a fence-lined track. Where the track bends left to a cottage, keep ahead along a grassy path to a gate. Go through and after crossing a track, continue along an enclosed path which heads downhill to emerge onto a lane. Turn right, continue downhill and where the lane bends right, turn left in front of the **Belle Monte Hotel** and almost

immediately bear right, at a public footpath sign, along a downhill path through woodland. At a fork a few yards ahead, take the left-hand path and you soon reach a fingerpost at another fork.

At this point the route continues along the left-hand upper path (signposted to Delamere and Beeston) but for the detour to **Frodsham church**, take the right-hand lower path, signposted to Frodsham Centre. After a sharp right bend, continue down steps and at the bottom turn right along a track to a road. Turn left down to Frodsham church, passing two pubs. The **Ring o' Bells** is opposite the church.

The parish church at Frodsham is situated above and some distance from the present town centre. There was a church recorded on the site in the Domesday Book and the present building dates from the 12th century but has been extensively enlarged, altered and rebuilt over the centuries, with a particularly comprehensive restoration in the Victorian era. The west tower was built during a 14th-century enlargement.

Retrace your steps up to the fork in the footpath at Point 2 and turn sharp right to continue on the main route. At the next Sandstone Trail post, turn left up a flight of steps, bending right and continuing up to the war memorial and **Mersey View**.

At a height of 443 ft, the views from here across the river Mersey, although perhaps too urban and industrial to be regarded as classically beautiful, are certainly both dramatic and extensive. On the horizon some of the buildings in Liverpool city centre can be seen, dominated inevitably by the tower of the city's Anglican cathedral.

From the viewpoint, keep ahead along a path, by a wire fence on the left, through gorse and bracken and, later, woodland. At a fork, take the right-hand lower path to continue along an undulating route through woodland across the face of **Woodhouse Hill**, following regular **Sandstone Trail** signs and passing some spectacular rock faces. There are more outstanding fine views, including some of the adjacent **Helsby Hill**.

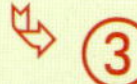 ③

At a fingerpost turn left, in the direction of the **Beacon Hill** car park, and after quickly emerging from the trees, continue in a straight line across a golf course. On the far side, keep ahead to a stile, climb it and head gently uphill along an enclosed sunken path to a lane. Turn right and the car park is just ahead.

PLACE OF INTEREST NEARBY

At the **Boat Museum** at Ellesmere Port, interactive galleries enable you to discover how the canals were built and the effects they had on the social and economic history of Britain. There are working engines, an extensive collection of canal boats, exhibitions and boat trips. There is also a coffee shop. The museum is signposted from junction 9 of the M53. Telephone: 0151 355 5017.

3 Dunham Park and the Bridgewater Canal

The Bridgewater Canal

Distance 3¾ miles **Terrain** Flat walking across parkland and along lanes and a canal towpath **Map** OS Explorer 276 Bolton, Wigan & Warrington (GR 733875)

How to get there

Dunham Massey is about 4 miles to the east of Lymm and 1½ miles west of Altrincham. The entrance to the park and house is off the B5160. **Parking**: National Trust pay car park at Dunham Massey.

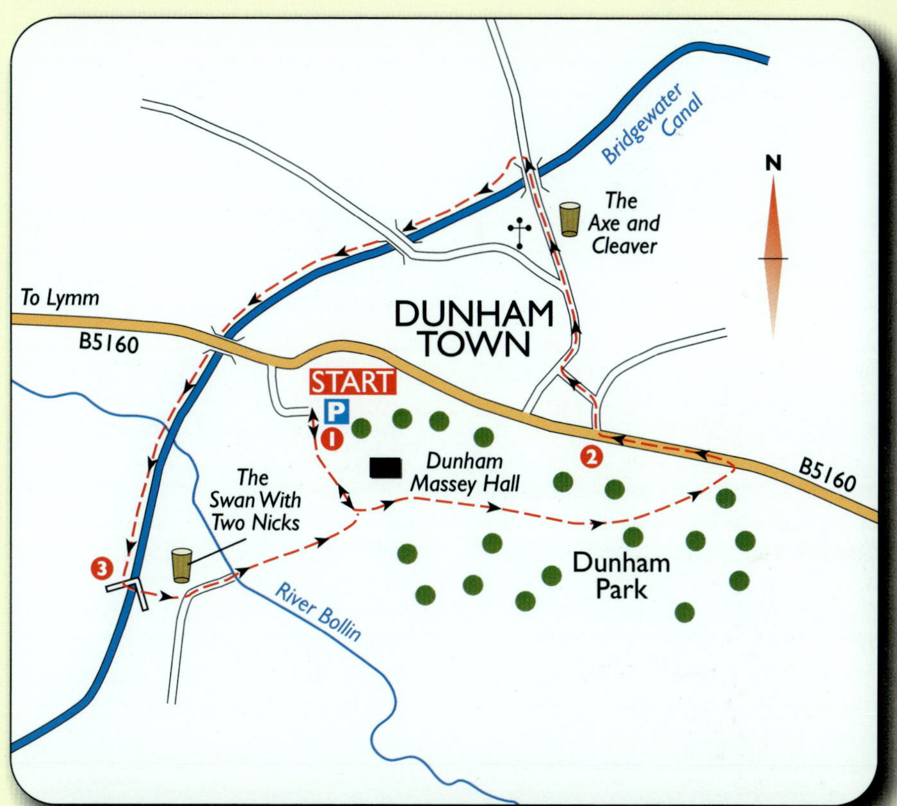

Introduction

The route falls into three main parts. The first is across the deer park at Dunham Massey, during which you may well be lucky enough to see some of the deer herd. Then comes a stretch along quiet lanes, followed by a pleasant and tranquil walk along a canal towpath, from which there are some fine views over the surrounding countryside. After that you briefly re-enter the deer park in order to return to the start. The paths and tracks are clear and easy to follow and the walking is flat throughout.

Refreshments

The walk passes two pubs, both of which do meals – the **Axe and Cleaver** north of Dunham Town just before reaching the canal, and the **Swan with Two Nicks** near the end just after leaving the canal. At the **Stables Restaurant** at Dunham Massey you can get morning coffee and afternoon teas and between 12 noon and 2 pm the restaurant provides cooked lunches, plus soup, sandwiches and mouth-watering sweets. Telephone: 0161 941 1025.

THE WALK

From the car park, turn left in front of the National Trust information hut and walk through trees along a tarmac track which bears right alongside a pool on the left to a gate. Go through, keep ahead and the track bends left around the end of a pool – to the right is the **Old Sawmill**. On joining another tarmac track, bear left. Over to the left is a fine view of the house.

The red brick Dunham Massey Hall has a long history. The original Tudor manor house was largely rebuilt in the 18th century on a more impressive scale by George Booth, 2nd Earl of Warrington. In the early 20th century this house was further remodelled. A tour of the hall includes the imposing library and long gallery and there is a fine collection of antique silver, furniture and paintings. In addition, visitors get a fascinating glimpse of life 'below stairs' in the servants' quarters. The Old Sawmill, passed just before reaching the hall, was originally a Tudor corn mill, converted into a sawmill in the Victorian period. It retains some of its working machinery.

The hall is surrounded by attractive gardens and stands in the midst of a large deer park that, as well as retaining its herd of deer, possesses some of the finest old trees in Cheshire. Nowadays both hall and park are owned and maintained by the National Trust. Telephone: 0161 941 1025.

At a fork in front of the house, take the right-hand track and continue across the deer park. After nearly ¾ mile, climb a ladder stile beside a lodge and turn left along a road, following the boundary wall of the park.

At a Dunham Massey sign turn right along **Charcoal Lane** to a T-junction in the village of **Dunham Town** and turn right again, passing the **Lavender Barn Tea Room**. Keep to the right of the small church and continue past the **Axe and Cleaver pub** to reach a canal bridge. Immediately after crossing it, turn left, at a public footpath sign, and head down a narrow enclosed path, turning left through a hedge gap onto the towpath of the **Bridgewater Canal**.

A pioneer of the 'Canal Age' at the start of the Industrial Revolution, the Bridgewater Canal claims to be the first real canal in Britain. It was built by James Brindley for the Duke of Bridgewater to carry coal from the duke's mines around Worsley to Manchester. It was opened in 1761 and was immediately successful, causing the price of coal in Manchester to fall by more than a half. By 1767 it had been extended to Runcorn to link Manchester to the river Mersey, making a total length of just under 40 miles.

Turn right and keep along the towpath for 1 mile.

Dunham Massey Hall

 ③

About ¼ mile after crossing the aqueduct over the **river Bollin** and just before reaching a sign on the opposite bank for the **Swan with Two Nicks**, bear right down steps to a track and turn sharp left, passing under an aqueduct. Walk along a track – which later becomes cobbled – to a lane and bear left, passing the Swan with Two Nicks. Where the lane ends, keep ahead to cross a footbridge over the Bollin, continue in front of a mill and where the tarmac track bends left, keep ahead beside a gate and continue along an enclosed tree-lined track. Climb a ladder stile to re-enter **Dunham Park** and at a junction, turn sharp left to rejoin your outward route by the **Old Sawmill**. Follow the track around a right bend and retrace your steps to the car park.

PLACE OF INTEREST NEARBY

Just a few miles away there is another deer park to explore at **Tatton**. This one has two good-sized lakes and two houses to visit, the early 16th-century Old Hall and its imposing 18th-century successor. Tatton Park lies on the edge of Knutsford and like Dunham Massey is owned by the National Trust. Telephone: 01565 654822.

4 Lindow Common and Styal Country Park

The view over Lindow Moss

Distance 5¾ miles **Terrain** Easy walking, mainly on field and woodland paths **Map** OS Explorer 268 Wilmslow, Macclesfield & Congleton (GR 834814)

How to get there

Lindow Common is just off the A538 on the western edge of Wilmslow. At the Boddington and Dragon inn, turn along Racecourse Road and the car park is to the left. **Parking**: Free car park at Lindow Common.

Introduction

Much of this attractive walk is through woods: first the delightful woodland that covers much of Lindow Common and surrounding area and later the woods around Styal that clothe the steep-sided banks of the river Bollin. The focal point of the route is the National Trust estate at Styal, a uniquely interesting example of a purpose-built 18th-century industrial community based around Quarry Bank Mill. Be sure to leave plenty of time to explore both the mill and Styal village.

Refreshments

The **Boddington and Dragon** at the start is a Thai restaurant but also has a traditional English bar menu offering a wide selection of full and light meals. You also pass the **Honey Bee pub** on the A538 between Morley and Quarry Bank Mill. The licensed café at **Quarry Bank Mill**, situated on the ground floor of the 18th-century building, serves morning coffee, soup, sandwiches, cooked lunches and afternoon teas. Telephone: 01625 527468.

THE WALK

Lindow Common is a most valuable amenity, a rare example of surviving lowland heath in Cheshire. Originally it mainly comprised open heathland and was used by local people for the grazing of animals. Now it is predominantly tree-covered but contains areas of both wet and dry heath, scrub and the beautiful Black Lake. In 1897 the common was given to the people of Wilmslow as a recreation area. A racecourse was built around the edge of it – hence Racecourse Road from which you entered the common – and children sailed boats on the lake. Now it is used for quieter activities, chiefly birdwatching and walking.

Begin by going through a kissing gate in the corner of the car park and follow a path across the wooded common. At a fork, take the left-hand sandy path which curves right to a T-junction in front of **Black Lake**. Turn right and just after the path follows the edge of the lake to the left, bear right onto a narrower path through trees and bushes to emerge into open heathland. Keep ahead at a crossways, re-enter woodland and go through a kissing gate onto a road.

Cross over and keep ahead along a broad tarmac track called **Lindow Lane**. At a public bridleway sign in front of a house, turn left along an enclosed track which curves right and continues in a straight line along the inside edge of woodland to reach a T-junction. Turn right along a track (**Rotherwood Road**) to the end of a lane and keep ahead along a tree-lined tarmac track, at a sign 'Bridlepath to Morley'. Over to the right is **Lindow Moss**.

Lindow Moss is an ancient peat bog which briefly hit the headlines in 1983 when the remains of a prehistoric man, later nicknamed Lindow Pete, were accidentally discovered there by peat diggers. Lindow Man is now on display at the British Museum in London.

At a crossways turn sharp right,

pass beside a barrier and continue along a tree-lined path. After about 200 yards, look out for a short waymarked post where you turn left onto an uphill path through trees. This attractive path runs across the middle of a former landfill site. The path later descends, bends right and continues through woodland to a gate. Go through and walk along an enclosed track to emerge onto a road at a junction. Keep ahead along **Morley Green Road** through the hamlet of Morley Green for nearly ¾ mile to the A538.

 ③

Turn right, passing the **Honey Bee pub** and, just after a right bend, turn left at a restricted byway sign, along an enclosed track. Go through two gates – the second one by farm buildings – and keep ahead along an enclosed path above the Bollin valley, between a line of trees on the right and a fence on the left. Go through a gate to enter the National Trust property of **Styal**, continue downhill and cross a bridge over the **river Bollin**. Head up beside **Quarry Bank Mill** and the path bends left and continues up to a tarmac track.

Quarry Bank Mill was built in 1784 by Samuel Greg, a Manchester cotton manufacturer, on the banks of the swift-flowing river Bollin close to the tiny farming hamlet of Styal near Wilmslow. At the time there was little here apart from a few black and white cottages for farm workers. The spinning mill

prospered and grew and in the 1830s Samuel's son Robert added some weaving sheds.

After years of prosperity Quarry Bank Mill declined after the First World War and in 1939 it was given – along with Styal village – to the National Trust. The mill is now a museum with a working waterwheel, demonstrations of textile machinery and displays on the conditions and way of life of the people who lived and worked here.

On the walk around the village, you can see some of the cottages that Samuel Greg built for his workers, the two chapels and, between the village and mill, you pass the Apprentice House, built around 1790 to house the pauper apprentices who were employed in the mill. The use of these as a source of cheap labour indicates that, although Samuel Greg was an enlightened employer by the standards of the time, he was still a hard-headed businessman and the working conditions at the mill were harsh with long hours, low pay and strict discipline.

The combination of Quarry Bank Mill and its associated buildings in Styal village gives visitors a unique insight into the functioning and way of life of an early Industrial Revolution mill community for both owners and workers. Telephone: 01625 527468.

 ④

The next part of the walk is a circuit of the village before returning to the mill. Keep ahead uphill along the track and at a sign to **Styal village**, turn left along an enclosed path. Keep ahead, going through four gates, and after the last of these you emerge onto a track to the left of **Styal Cross**. Ahead are some of Samuel Greg's cottages for his workers and to the left is **Norcliffe Chapel**. Turn right, at a fork take the right-hand path to the Methodist chapel and turn right onto a cobbled track. Keep ahead through a gate, walk along a hedge-lined track and at a house, turn right through a gate and pass in front of the **Apprentice House**. On joining a tarmac track you briefly rejoin the previous route and continue down to pass in front of **Quarry Bank Mill**.

Go through a gate beyond the mill buildings and continue along an enclosed tarmac path through trees by the **river Bollin** on the right. Keep on this path, at one stage turning right over **Herons Pool Bridge**, after which you continue by woodland to a fork. Take the left-hand path, go through a kissing gate on the edge of the trees and keep ahead across a grassy area, bearing right on joining another path and making for a kissing gate on the far side. Go through, turn right along a tarmac track, cross a bridge over the river and keep ahead to a car park.

At a restricted byway sign, turn right to re-cross the **Bollin** and keep ahead along a track through woodland, heading gently uphill to a gate. Pass beside it onto the end of a road and turn left along a track. At another restricted byway sign turn right onto a winding, fence-lined path which emerges onto a tarmac drive. Keep ahead, continue along an enclosed track to a road and turn right. At a T-junction turn left along **Kings Road** to the A538, cross carefully – this is a busy stretch of road – and take the broad, tree-lined track ahead. At the next road, turn left to return to the start.

PLACE OF INTEREST NEARBY

Arley Hall, a grand Victorian country house built in the style of an Elizabethan mansion, is particularly noted for its beautiful gardens and woodland walks. There is an old chapel, gift shop and a restaurant housed in a medieval barn. The hall and gardens lie between Northwich and Warrington and are signposted from the A559. Telephone: 01565 777353.

5 Alderley Edge

Looking across the Cheshire Plain

Distance 2½ miles **Terrain** Woodland paths and tracks
Map OS Explorer 268 Wilmslow, Macclesfield & Congleton (GR 860773)

How to get there

From the A34 at Alderley Edge, take the B5087 and the car park is on the left about 1½ miles from the village. **Parking**: National Trust pay car park at Alderley Edge.

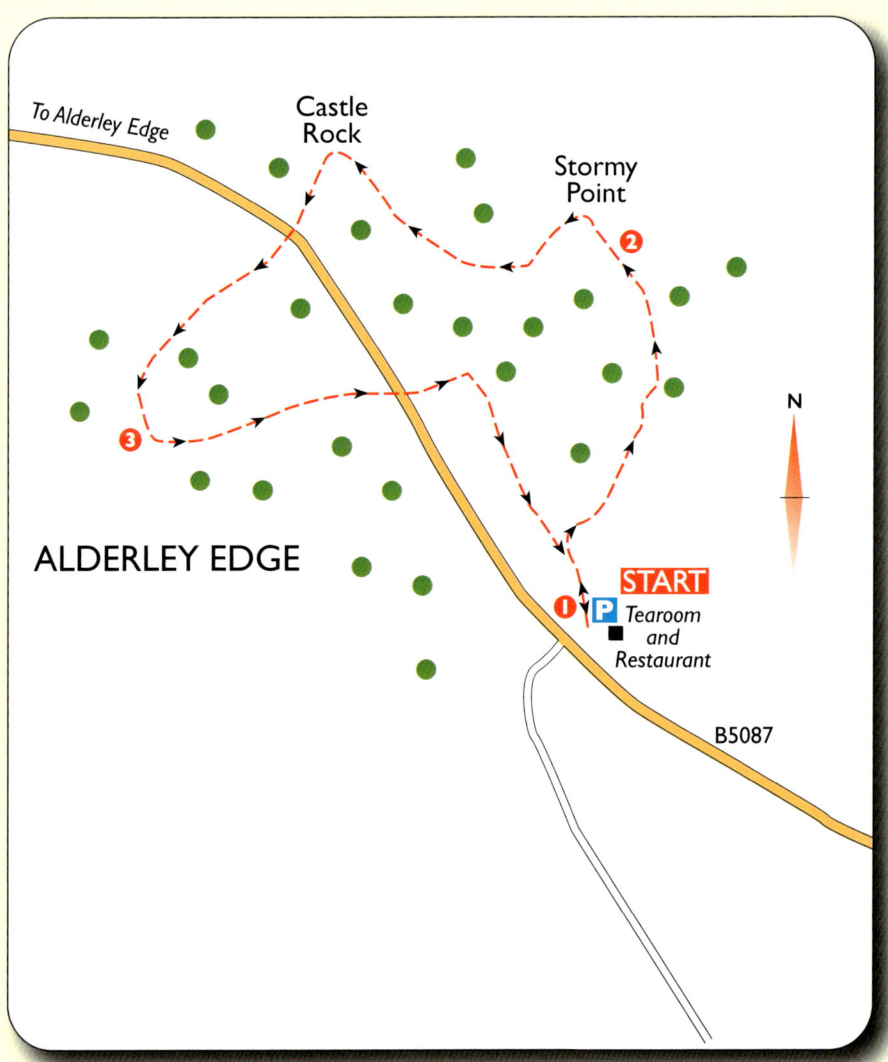

Introduction

Although a short walk and predominantly through woodland, there is plenty of interest, beauty and variety. The woodland is highly attractive, there are several magnificent viewpoints and areas of more open landscapes, plus a number of reminders of the history and geology of this part of Cheshire. The whole of the route is on National Trust land.

Refreshments

There is a tearoom and restaurant at the start of the walk although the **Wizard Tea Room** is only open on weekends and Bank Holiday Mondays between 10 am and 5 pm. The **Wizard of Edge restaurant** provides a good choice of main meals and lighter options in pleasant and relaxing surroundings. It is closed on Mondays. Telephone: 01625 584000.

THE WALK

Alderley Edge is the prominent sandstone escarpment that rises more than 600 ft above the Cheshire plain. Its steep and thickly-wooded slopes are covered with thick oak and beech woodland and from a number of gaps in the trees, there are magnificent views across the plain to the hills of the Peak District on the horizon.

As the names of both the tearoom and restaurant indicate, the area is closely associated with wizard legends. There are several of these but they are all basically slight variations on the same theme. The story goes that one day a local farmer was approached by an old man who offered to buy his white horse. As they walked along the Edge, the old man tapped with his stick on the ground and a pair of iron gates suddenly appeared. On walking through these gates, the farmer saw hundreds of men and white horses lying asleep and was told by the old man that they were waiting there ready to fight to save England when needed. Another version states that the wizard was Merlin and the sleeping men were King Arthur's Knights of the Round Table.

Until the middle of the 19th century this was a sparsely populated area and Alderley Edge was simply the name of a geographical feature. The arrival of the railway led to the rapid expansion of the local village of Chorley as a desirable residential area for Manchester businessmen and industrialists and in order to avoid confusion with the town of Chorley in Lancashire, the railway company renamed it Alderley Edge.

At a sign 'Footpaths' in the car park, take the hedge-lined path to a T-junction. The information centre, tearoom and restaurant are to the left; the route is to the right along a track, signposted to **Hare Hill**. The track curves left and at a sharp right bend, keep ahead through a gate - there is a yellow waymark – and walk along a wide track through woodland. Soon you emerge into an open area at the magnificent viewpoint of **Stormy Point**.

From these sandstone outcrops you enjoy one of the grandest views in Cheshire extending across the

The site of Engine Vein mine

Cheshire plain to the distant buildings of Stockport and Manchester. On a clear day, the line of the Pennines and the hills and moors of the Peak District are visible on the horizon.

 ②

From **Stormy Point**, turn sharp left along a path, in the direction of an orange waymark. At a fork, take the right-hand path and at the next fork, head up to a yellow-waymarked post at the corner of a wall on the left. Continue along a path which later keeps by the left edge of the trees to reach a rocky outcrop called **Castle Rock**, another superb viewpoint. Follow the path around a left bend and continue to the road.

Cross over, climb a stile opposite, at a public footpath sign, and walk along the left edge of a field. After climbing a stile, continue along a most attractive tree-lined path to a T-junction and turn left. At a fork take the right-hand path and look out for a half-hidden orange waymarker post where you bear left and continue along a path to a T-junction. For the remainder of the walk you follow the regular orange waymarks.

 ③

Turn left, bear left at the next waymarked post and in front of an Alderley Edge National Trust sign, bear right and head gently uphill. Take the left-hand path at a fork and on emerging into an open area, bear right along a path to reach the road again. Cross over, keep ahead into the trees and, at a fork, continue along the left-hand path to a crossways. Turn right and on the left you pass the **Engine Vein mine**.

Engine Vein is the best-known, most obvious and most impressive of the many former mine workings that litter the Edge. For centuries Alderley Edge has been extensively mined and quarried and claims to be the oldest known site of metal mining in the country. Copper, lead and other metals were extracted here from prehistoric times up to the early 20th century and the greatest concentration of old mining features and artefacts – the lines of ancient mine shafts and tools dating from the Bronze Age and Roman periods – have been found at Engine Vein. In 1995 a hoard of Roman coins dating from the 4th century AD were found here in a pot in one of the old shafts. The present workings that can be seen near the surface are much later, probably from the 18th century.

Continue along the path to reach the track near the tearoom and pub. Cross it and take the path ahead to return to the car park.

PLACE OF INTEREST NEARBY

There is plenty to interest all members of the family at the **Jodrell Bank Observatory**, signposted from the A535 between Alderley Edge and Holmes Chapel. As well as walking round and admiring the giant Lovell Telescope (there are plenty of information boards), you can observe the stars and solar system in the film theatre at the Visitor Centre, visit the Environmental Discovery Centre and take a relaxing walk through the Granada Arboretum. There is also a shop and café. Telephone: 01477 571339.

6 Lyme Park

Distance 3½ miles **Terrain** Tarmac drives and woodland paths, plus some rough walking across grassland and moorland **Map** OS Explorer OL1 The Peak District – Dark Peak Area (GR 963824)

How to get there

The entrance to Lyme Park is off the A6 about ½ mile to the west of Disley and about 6½ miles to the south-east of Stockport. **Parking:** Pay car park at Lyme Park.

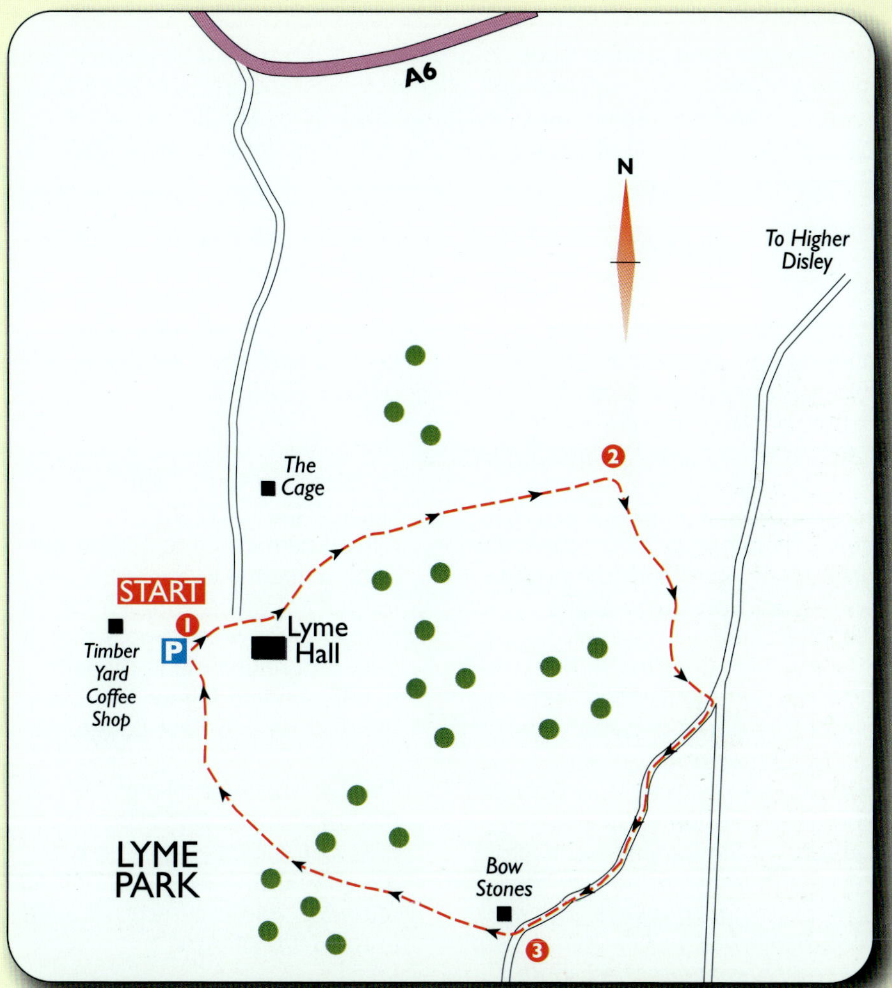

Introduction

This walk on the western fringes of the Peak District takes you mainly through the parkland surrounding a great house. It starts by the house and heads first across the deer park and later over rough grassland, climbing up to the highest point on the route at the Bow Stones. From this point, at around 1300 ft, there are superb and extensive views. The descent back to the start takes you across open moorland and through woodland, from where you enjoy some fine views of the house.

Refreshments

The **Timber Yard Coffee Shop** is a short walk from the car park. It does morning coffee, light lunches and afternoon teas and the lunches include soup, sandwiches, cakes and several cooked items. In fine weather it is pleasant to sit outside at the courtyard tables. Telephone: 01663 762023.

THE WALK

Lyme Park was originally an outlying part of Macclesfield Forest and was enclosed around the middle of the 14th century as a deer park. In 1398 Richard II gave it to the Legh family as a reward for service in the Hundred Years' War and it remained in their possession until 1946 when both the house and estate were given to the National Trust.

In the 16th century Sir Piers Legh built a grand Elizabethan mansion on the site of the previous modest medieval manor house. This mansion was considerably enlarged and altered in the early 18th century by the Venetian architect Leoni who transformed it in the style of an Italian palace. His work is particularly noted for the elegant and much photographed south front. A period of neglect was followed by more changes in the early 19th century when Lewis Wyatt restored the house, redesigned much of the interior and added the tower above Leoni's south front.

A tour of the state rooms reveals a wealth of paintings, tapestries and furniture, plus a large number of clocks collected by the Leghs. Visitors can also visit the orangery which adjoins the house and enjoy the colourful 19th-century gardens. Telephone: 01663 762023.

From the car park, head up the steps to the left of the refreshment and information hut to the entrance to the house. In front of the gates, turn left onto a tarmac drive which bends right to a fork. Continue along the left-hand drive and follow it across the deer park to **East Lodge**.

The tall isolated building seen to the left is called The Cage. It was built in the Elizabethan period, possibly as a viewing platform for the hunt, and was reconstructed in the 18th century.

At the lodge go through a gate to leave the park and keep ahead along an enclosed path.

At a fingerpost, turn right over a stile, in the **Bow Stones** direction, and walk across rough grassland to a waymarked post. Continue beyond it to the next post, bear first left and then right and walk across a field to go through a kissing gate in the far left-hand corner. Bear slightly left through a group of trees into a dip and turn left to another kissing gate. Go through, immediately turn right and head uphill, by a fence on the right, towards farm buildings. Before reaching them bear left, go through a gate beside a barn and walk through the farmyard, turning left to a gate. Go through, keep ahead along a tarmac track and go through a gate onto a road at a junction. Turn right and right again along a lane signposted to Bow Stones – there is also a No Through Road sign – and head uphill to the **Bow Stones** at the top.

The Bow Stones are the remains of two Anglo-Saxon crosses that may have been placed here in the 16th century as boundary markers. The views from here extend over the hills and moorlands of the western Peak District to the distinctive outline of Shutlingsloe, the 'Cheshire Matterhorn' and across the built-up area of Greater Manchester.

The Bow Stones

 ③

Just beyond the **Bow Stones**, turn right over a stile, at a **Gritstone Trail** sign, and walk along the right field edge to a ladder stile. Climb it – here re-entering **Lyme Park** – and keep ahead across open moorland, heading downhill towards the edge of woodland. Go through a gate, keep ahead through the trees, go through another gate on the far edge of the wood and continue downhill by the left edge of trees to a kissing gate. Go through and keep ahead along a tarmac track to return to the car park.

PLACE OF INTEREST NEARBY

Bramall Hall is another fine country house near Stockport. Situated off the A5102, about 4 miles south of Stockport, it is one of Cheshire's grand black and white, timber-framed houses. The oldest parts date back to the 14th century but the house is mostly Tudor with Victorian additions. There is a gift shop and tearoom. Telephone: 0161 485 3708.

7 Wildboarclough and Shutlingsloe

The view to Cheshire's 'Matterhorn'

Distance 3½ miles, or 2½ if you omit the climb to the summit of Shutlingsloe **Terrain** A combination of lanes, easy tracks and some rough paths, two climbs but the short but steep and rocky ascent to the summit of Shutlingsloe can be avoided if desired **Map** OS Explorer OL24 The Peak District – White Peak Area (GR 987699)

How to get there

Clough House car park is on the narrow road that runs through the deep valley of Clough Brook to the south-east of Macclesfield. Follow signs to Wildboarclough from either the A537 to the north or A54 to the south. **Parking**: Peak National Park car park at Clough House (free).

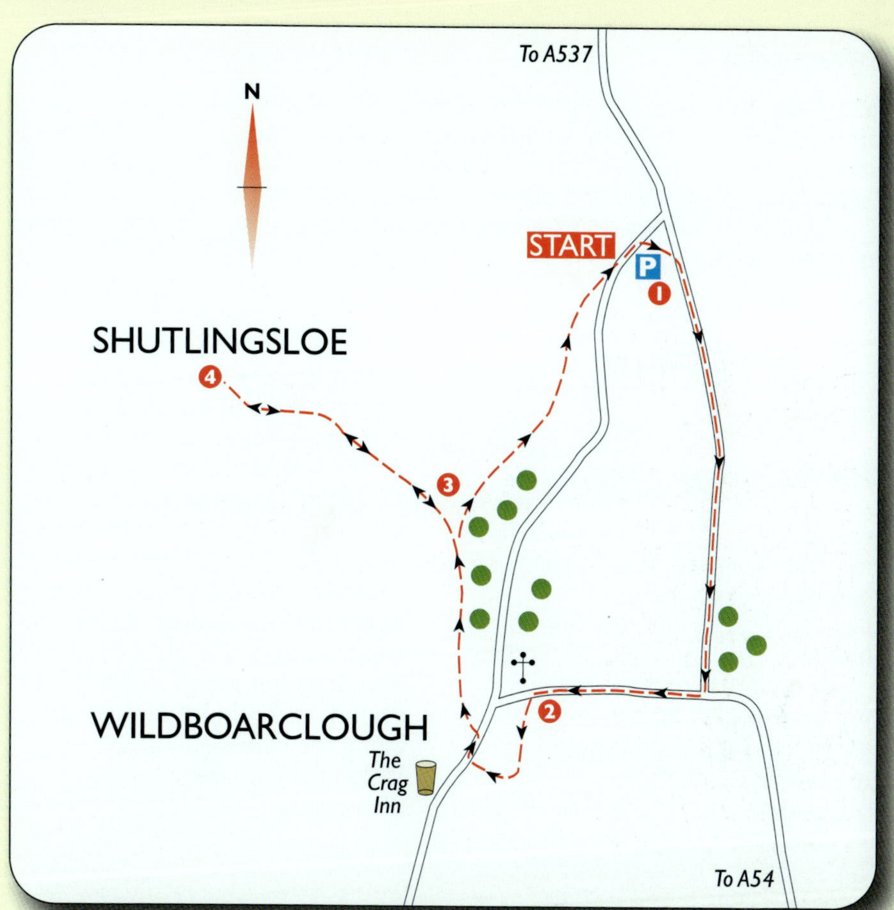

Introduction

There are stunning views both of and from Shutlingsloe, the Cheshire 'Matterhorn', on this route. An undulating opening section along lanes and paths, passing the little church at Wildboarclough, is followed by an easy climb onto the lower slopes of the hill. From here a steep path – rocky in its later stages – leads up to the summit, a magnificent all round viewpoint. You descend by the same route and continue above the valley of Clough Brook before gently descending back to the start. The 'there and back' path to the summit can be omitted by those walkers not keen on a steep climb to an exposed hilltop, but if you have the energy, time and inclination – and the weather is reasonably fine – it is definitely to be recommended.

Refreshments

The **Crag Inn** gets its name because it sits at the foot of the crag of Shutlingsloe. The building was previously a farm called Bottom o' th Bank and became a pub in the early 19th century. It is a cosy little country pub, complete with log fires, and offers a range of cooked and light meals. There is a carvery on Sunday. In fine weather you can enjoy the surrounding views from the outdoor seating area. Telephone: 01260 227239.

THE WALK

Begin by walking through the car park and on along a tarmac track which curves left up to a lane. Turn right uphill. As the lane flattens out, there are striking views of the distinctive summit of Shutlingsloe to the right. The lane later descends to a fork. Take the right-hand lane (signposted to Wildboarclough and Wincle) and continue downhill to **St Saviour's church** at Wildboarclough.

This small and tucked away church is not as old as it looks. It was built in the early years of the 20th century by the Earl of Derby, the local landowner, as a memorial and thanksgiving for the safe return of his sons from the Boer War. It merges perfectly into its surroundings, perhaps because it was built from local stone by mainly local estate workers.

At the church the lane bears left. At a public footpath sign, turn left along an enclosed tarmac drive. Continue along a rough track to where it ends at a wall, climb a stone stile in the wall and walk across a field. On the far side, turn right alongside a wall on the left, climb a stile and continue downhill by the left inside edge of woodland. Ford a stream, cross a footbridge over **Clough Brook** and climb a stone stile onto a lane. The **Crag Inn** is just to the left. The route continues to the right along the lane. At a public footpath sign, bear left uphill along an enclosed tarmac track.

At a fork, *those walkers who do not wish to climb* to the summit of Shutlingsloe should take the right-hand track and pick up the route directions from where point 3 appears next in the text.
For those doing the full walk, climb the stile in front and continue uphill along the left-hand tarmac track. Where it curves right to a farm, keep ahead and go through a wall gap. Head more steeply uphill, climbing two stiles, and continue

up towards the summit. On reaching the rocky area just below the summit cone, the path – now less obvious – swings left and you pick your way between the boulders, finally bending right to emerge onto the top at the trig point.

St Saviour's church

It is the distinctive appearance of Shutlingsloe that has earned it the nickname of the 'Cheshire Matterhorn'. It rises to a height of 1,659 ft and is a magnificent all-round viewpoint. In fine weather the views extend over the rolling hills and exposed moors of the Peak District and across the Cheshire plain to Greater Manchester, Merseyside and – in particularly clear conditions – the hills of North Wales.

 ④

Retrace your steps down to where the track forks (**point 3**). Turn sharp left through a gate and walk along a track by a wall on the right bordering steeply sloping woodland. Where this track ends, climb a stone stile and keep ahead on a path that runs along the side of the valley, descending gently to a gate. Go through, keep ahead and climb a stile onto a lane. Turn left and the starting point is about 100 yards ahead.

PLACE OF INTEREST NEARBY

Capesthorne Hall is situated off the A34 between Alderley Edge and Congleton and about 5 miles west of Macclesfield. This grand 18th-century house, ancestral home of the Bromley-Davenport family, had to be extensively rebuilt in the Victorian era following a disastrous fire in 1861. Despite this, it contains a fine collection of antique furniture, paintings and tapestries. As well as the house, you can enjoy the gardens and grounds with their woodland walks and lakes. Telephone: 01625 861221.

8 Tegg's Nose and Macclesfield Forest

Looking towards Shutlingsloe

Distance 5½ miles **Terrain** Mainly a mixture of conifer woodland and open moorland **Map** OS Explorer OL24 The Peak District – White Peak Area (GR 960733)

How to get there SK11 ØAP.

Tegg's Nose Country Park is about 2½ miles from Macclesfield. Take the A537 towards Buxton and the road to it leads off to the right soon after leaving the town centre. **Parking**: Pay and display car park at Tegg's Nose Country Park.

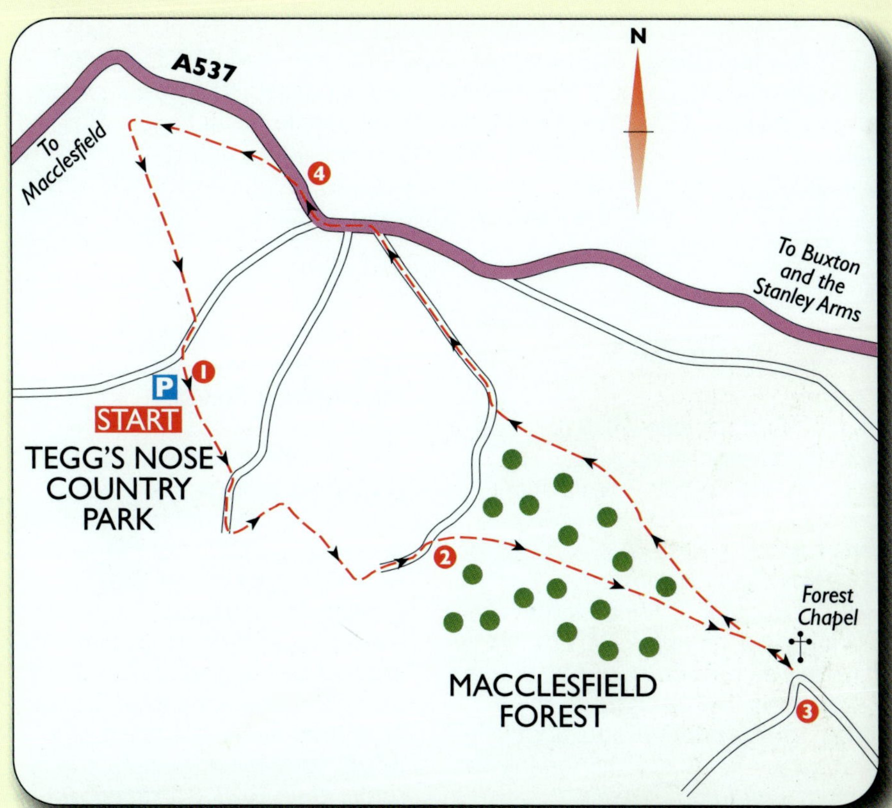

Introduction

From the elevated viewpoint of Tegg's Nose, you descend into the valley and follow tracks and paths to the edge of Macclesfield Forest. The next stage of the route is through dense conifer plantations to the Forest Chapel. A gradual ascent along first a track and then a lane brings you to the A537. On the final stretch along the Gritstone Trail there are extensive views over the surrounding moorland, with Tegg's Nose and the distinctive outline of Shutlingsloe both prominent.

Refreshments

The **Stanley Arms** is situated in a part of Macclesfield Forest quaintly known as the Bottom of the Oven. It gets its name from an old packhorse trail called Oven Lane, the original road between Buxton and Macclesfield, which crossed Clough Brook near here. To reach it from Tegg's Nose, take the A537 towards Buxton and turn right along the minor road to Wildboarclough. This splendid inn has just about everything: open fires, good views, excellent and varied food and a cosy atmosphere. It has a wide menu ranging from full cooked meals to sandwiches and has a separate dining room. It is particularly famous for its Bottom of the Oven lamb which allegedly attracts visitors from all over the country and from abroad. Telephone: 01260 252414.

THE WALK

Tegg's Nose Country Park occupies a steep hillside overlooking Macclesfield Forest. From it there are spectacular views over the forest and the western moorlands of the Peak District, with the distinctive peak of Shutlingsloe standing out prominently. The hillside was previously quarried and a path from the car park to the 'nose' itself – another outstanding viewpoint – leads past old quarry workings and equipment.

From the car park take the downhill track, signposted **Saddlers Way**. The track later becomes paved and descends quite steeply to a lane. Continue downhill and after a sharp left bend, the lane becomes first an enclosed uphill track and later a path. After a right bend, head downhill, ford a stream at the bottom and continue up again. At the top, turn left at a waymarked post along another enclosed path. In front of a farm turn right along a lane. Immediately after a left bend,

turn right over a stile at a public footpath sign to enter **Macclesfield Forest**.

The present Macclesfield Forest comprises a block of conifer plantations, moorland and reservoirs spread over the western slopes of the Peak District. In medieval times it was a large royal hunting ground, created by the Earl of Chester, and covered a somewhat greater area than today but much of it would have been open moorland rather than thick woodland. It is now owned by United Utilities.

Follow the path ahead through the conifers to a T-junction. Turn right, in the **Forest Chapel** direction. On emerging into a clearing by a ruined building, bear left to a footpath post at a crossways. Keep ahead, climb a stile and continue in the Forest Chapel direction along a path that heads uphill – there are steps at regular intervals – and eventually emerges from the trees at a gate. Go through the gate, turn right

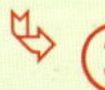

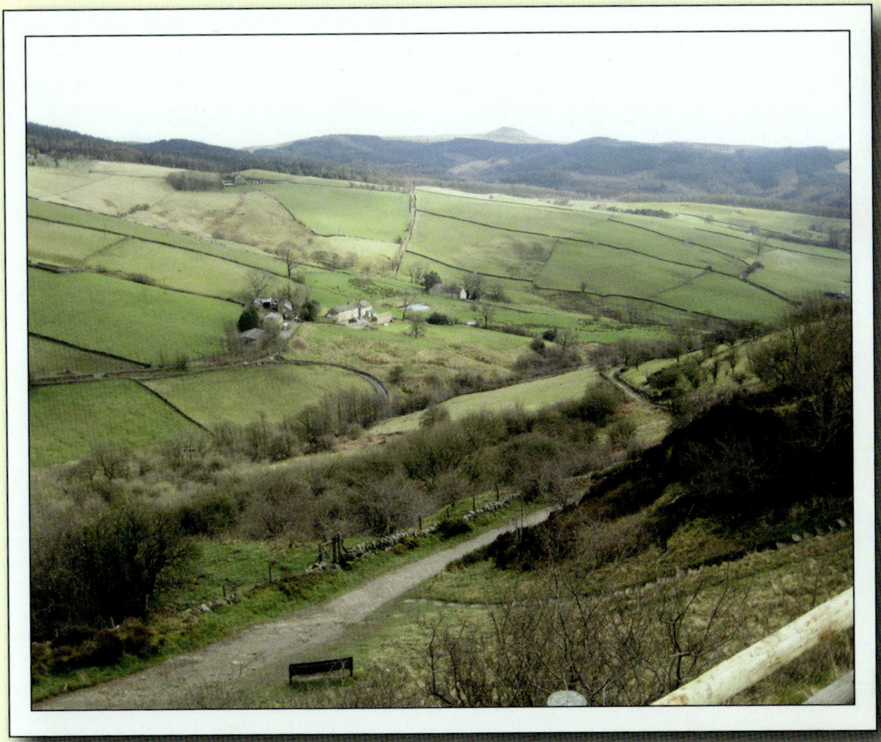

The rolling countryside seen from the path

along a track and head gently downhill to a junction of lanes. The **Forest Chapel** is just a few yards to the left.

The small and simple church of St Stephen, built in 1673 and reconstructed in 1831, is nearly always referred to as the Forest Chapel. It is well known as one of the churches where an annual rushbearing ceremony is held. Traditionally this was to commemorate the laying of new rushes on the floor of the church to provide a clean and dry surface, an event that came to symbolize annual renewal.

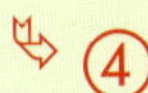

③

Retrace your steps up the track and continue along it by the right edge of the forest to reach a lane. Turn right and the lane bends left and heads down to the **A537**. Turn left and follow the road around a right bend.

④

At a public footpath sign – just by the 'Welcome to Macclesfield' sign – bear left along an uphill tarmac

track to a gate. Go through, continue along the track which curves gradually left to another gate. After going through it, keep ahead between farm buildings, go through another gate and continue along an enclosed track. After the next gate, keep by the right field edge, climb a stone stile and continue along the right edge of the next field.

In the field corner turn left, here joining the **Gritstone Trail**, and head uphill along a path which keeps parallel to the right field edge to a stile. After climbing it, the way continues along a clear and well-signed path across a series of fields and through a succession of gates and stiles, initially climbing gently and later descending across the final field to a stone stile. Climb it, turn left along a track to a road and turn right to return to the start.

PLACE OF INTEREST NEARBY

Gawsworth Hall, a typical black and white Cheshire building, is situated about 3 miles south of Macclesfield just off the A536. It dates mainly from the 15th and 16th centuries and is surrounded by attractive gardens and parkland. The views of the hall and nearby church from across the lake are superb. Telephone: 01260 223456.

9 | Three Shires Head

The packhorse bridge at Three Shires Head

Distance 6½ miles **Terrain** Mostly moorland tracks and paths, with some lane walking towards the end; some muddy stretches likely, mainly by the river between the A54 and Three Shires Head **Map** OS Explorer OL24 The Peak District – White Peak Area (GR 002719)

How to get there

The Cat & Fiddle Inn is situated on the A537 approximately halfway between Macclesfield and Buxton. **Parking:** Parking spaces opposite the Cat & Fiddle.

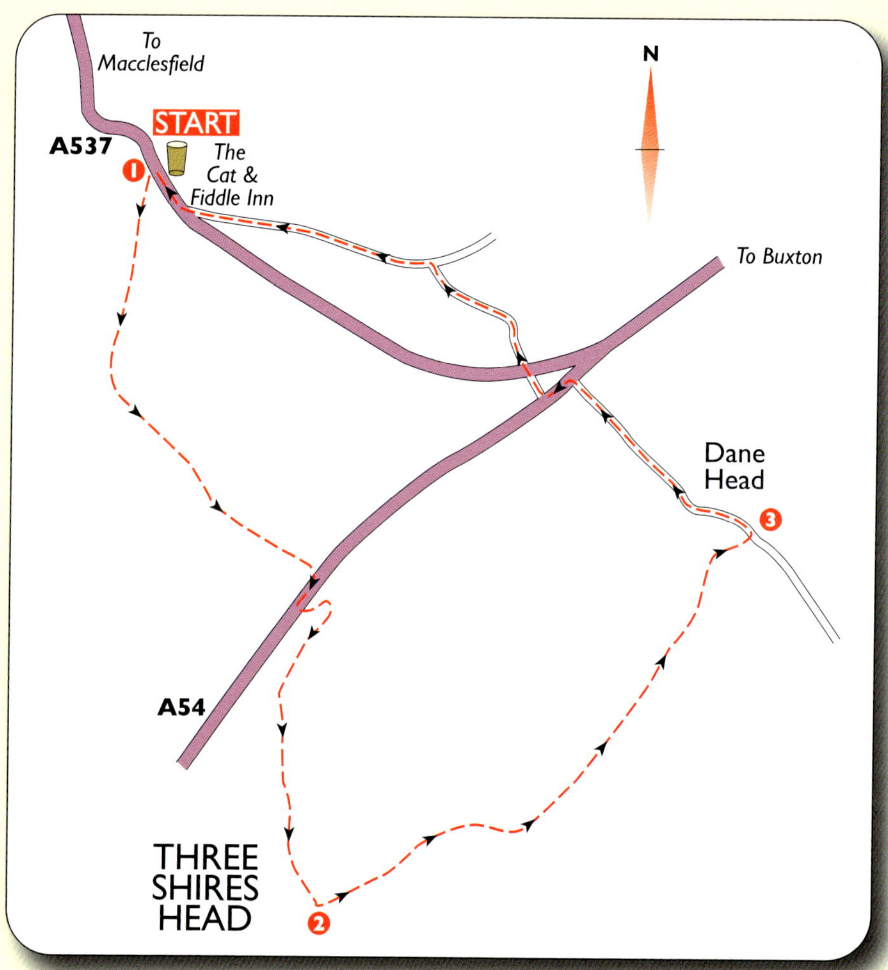

Introduction

Starting almost 1,700 ft up on open and exposed moorland, the route descends into the valley of the river Dane and continues by the infant river to the remote but popular beauty spot of Three Shires Head. A long and steady climb across more open moorland tracks brings you to Dane Head and from there quiet lanes lead back to the start. As some of the paths are not always clear on the ground, it is best to choose a reasonably fine day for this walk, unless you are an experienced moorland walker, in order to be able to pick out the landmarks and enjoy the extensive views at their best.

Refreshments

For many years the thick walls of the **Cat & Fiddle Inn** have given hospitality to travellers of all kinds – motorists, cyclists and walkers – seeking refuge from the sometimes inclement weather at this exposed spot. On cold winter days its open fires are a particularly welcoming sight and the inn provides an extensive range of cooked lunches, including a Sunday afternoon carvery, light meals (soup and sandwiches) with vegetarian options and a children's menu. Meals can be eaten either in the bar or the separate dining room. Telephone: 01298 23364.

THE WALK

Standing at a height of 1,690 ft, the Cat & Fiddle Inn is situated at the highest point on the Macclesfield to Buxton road amidst the bare, austere but undeniably beautiful moorlands of the Peak District. Not surprisingly it commands extensive views in all directions. It is the second highest pub in England, surpassed only by the Tan Hill Inn in the northern Pennines, and dates back to the early 19th century.

At a public bridleway sign opposite the pub, take the track across open moorland. Go through a gate, keep ahead and at a public footpath sign, continue along the main track which gradually descends to the A54. Go through a gate, turn right along the road for about 100 yards and at a public footpath sign, turn sharp left along a track above the valley of the infant **river Dane**. Shortly after going through a gate

and just after passing a chimney below on the right, turn right down to the chimney and head steeply down past it to a gate. Go through and continue through the valley, following the twists and turns of the river on the left and climbing a series of stiles, to reach the footbridge over **Panniers Pool** at **Three Shires Head**.

As its name suggests, Three Shires Head is the meeting place of three counties – Cheshire, Derbyshire and Staffordshire. The combination of two old packhorse bridges, gushing streams, rocky outcrops and expanses of bracken and heather makes this an exceptionally beautiful and atmospheric place, enhanced by its sense of remoteness. In fine weather it is an ideal spot for a drink or picnic break.

Turn left over the footbridge, go through a gate and keep ahead along a path above a stream on the right. At a footpath sign just in front

The Cat & Fiddle pub

of a gate, turn left along a path signposted to **Orchard Common**, go through a gate, keep ahead and the path heads up to emerge onto a tarmac track. Continue steadily uphill along the track to a T-junction, turn left along a stony track and where this track curves left, keep ahead to a gate. Go through, continue steadily uphill across the open moorland and go through another gate. Veer slightly left to keep by a wire fence on the left and at the fence corner, continue ahead, climbing gently to a footpath post seen in front.

 ③

Turn left along a narrow lane to **Dane Head** and keep along this to the A54. Turn left and take the first lane on the right to the A537. Cross over and continue along the lane opposite which descends into a hollow and bends left to reach a T-junction. Turn left for one last climb to rejoin the A537 and turn right to return to the start.

PLACES OF INTEREST NEARBY

In the centre of Macclesfield there are three silk museums in close proximity to each other - the **Silk Industry Museum**, **Paradise Mill** and the **Heritage Centre**. Together they tell the history of the silk industry in Macclesfield from the early 19th century to the present day through displays, films and examples of machinery. At the Heritage Centre there is a shop and restaurant. Tel: 01625 612045.

10 The Cloud

The summit of The Cloud

Distance 4 miles **Terrain** A steady climb along clear paths and tracks to a summit followed by an easy descent. Much of the return leg is along a lane and road. **Map** OS Explorer 268 Wilmslow, Macclesfield & Congleton (GR 895627)

How to get there

Timbersbrook is signposted from the A54 just to the east of Congleton town centre. **Parking:** Free car park at Timbersbrook picnic area.

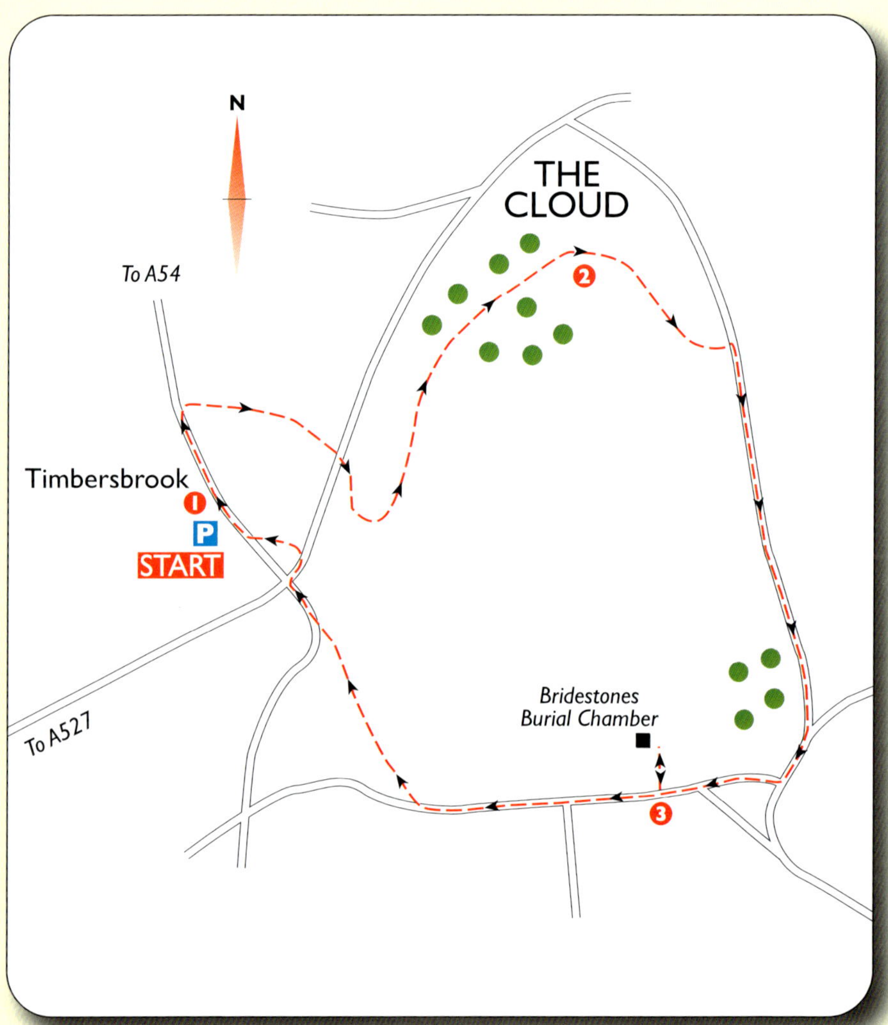

Introduction

The Cloud is the prominent hill that lies a few miles to the east of Congleton. A steady climb, partly through attractive woodland and the last stretch across open moorland, leads to the 1,125-ft summit, a superb viewpoint and, in fine weather, a glorious picnic spot. An easy descent is followed by flat walking along a lane, road and footpaths to return to the start. On this latter part of the route you pass an impressive prehistoric burial site.

Refreshments

The **Coach and Horses** is about 1 mile to the south-west of Timbersbrook along the lane signposted to Congleton. The location of the pub is most attractive with fine views over the surrounding countryside. On cold days there is an open fire and the garden can be used when the weather is suitable. A full range of cooked lunches and lighter meals is provided every day of the week. Telephone: 01260 273019.

THE WALK

Nowadays the Timbersbrook picnic area is a tranquil spot but this was not always so as it occupies the site of a former silk mill and dye works and there were quarries in the vicinity. The industries were attracted here in Victorian times by the power provided by the fast flowing brook. Foremost among them was the Silversprings Bleaching and Dye Company established in the early 20th century. At its height it employed over 200 workers but closed down in 1961. The building was demolished in 1976.

Turn right out of the car park along the road and after about one-third mile turn right, at a public bridleway sign, along a tree-lined track called **Acorn Lane**. Initially you head gently uphill and later continue more steeply up to a road. Cross over, continue along the uphill track opposite through woodland (**Gosberryhole Lane**). Follow the track around a left bend and head up to a fork. Take the left-hand track, following both **Gritstone Trail** and **Staffordshire Way** signs. Pass beside a barrier at a National Trust sign saying 'The Cloud', and continue up through trees to a T-junction. Turn left, then curve right and continue up to a fence. Pass beside the fence to a junction of tracks and, following the direction of Gritstone Trail and Staffordshire Way signs, keep ahead uphill through woodland. Eventually you emerge from the trees onto open, heathery moorland and continue along a winding, rocky path which heads gently uphill to the trig point and viewfinder on the summit of **The Cloud**.

At a height of 1,125 ft, The Cloud is both a magnificent and contrasting viewpoint. The views take in Congleton and Macclesfield, the moors and hills of the western Peak District and the wide expanses of the Cheshire plain, with the giant telescope at Jodrell Bank inevitably prominent.

At the trig point the path turns right

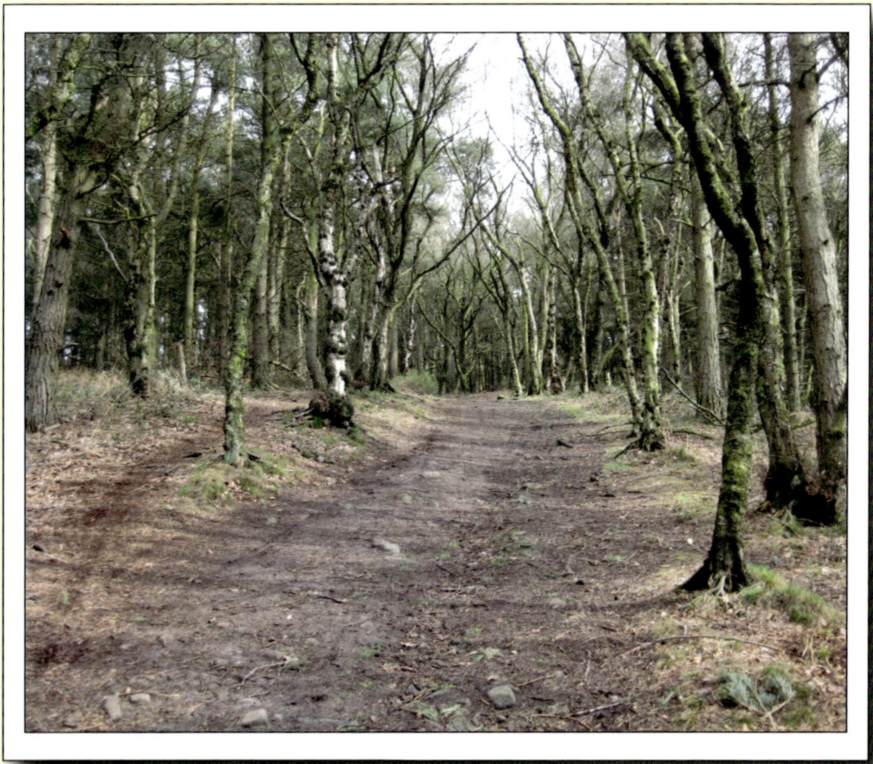

along the ridge and heads gently downhill to a fence. Pass beside it, continue along an enclosed path and descend a flight of steps to a track. Turn left and the track bends sharp right and continues down to a lane. Turn right and after about ¾ mile, take the first lane on the right which curves left to a road. Turn right and look out for a public footpath sign on the right.

 ③

Here a short detour along a tarmac track to the right leads to the **Bridestones Burial Site**.

The present remains are but a fragment of the large Neolithic chambered tomb that was built here. It was originally over 100 yards long and had three chambers. Over the centuries the tomb has been extensively exploited as a convenient quarry and many of the stones have been used in the building of local farms and roads. Despite this it is still an impressive monument, the oldest in Cheshire, a county not noted for the quality or quantity of its prehistoric sites.

Continue along the straight road for just over ½ mile – take care as there is not much of a verge at times – and at a public footpath sign by farm buildings, turn right through a gate. Climb the stile immediately in front and bear gradually left across a field, making for the far left-hand corner where you continue by a wire fence on the right. Go through a gap between a hedge and wall and continue along an undulating path above **Timbers Brook**, by a hedge on the right, to a stile. Climb it, keep ahead along the left edge of the next field and in the corner on the edge of woodland, turn left and descend to cross a footbridge over the brook. Head uphill, climb a stile onto a road and turn right. At a fork take the right-hand road and when you see a flight of steps on the left, descend them and follow a winding path through the picnic area back to the car park.

PLACE OF INTEREST NEARBY

Salt has been produced in Cheshire for over 2,000 years and it is appropriate that the **Salt Museum** at **Northwich** is located in the heartland of the industry. After an introductory film, a tour of the galleries reveals the fascinating history of the industry, the lives of the people who worked in it and the multitude of uses for salt throughout the world. The museum, housed in a former workhouse, is on the A533, ½ mile south of Northwich town centre. Telephone: 01606 41331.

11 | Mow Cop and the Macclesfield Canal

The Macclesfield Canal below Mow Cop

Distance 4 miles **Terrain** Clear paths, one ascent and descent, canal towpath, some muddy stretches likely after rain **Map** OS Explorer 268 Wilmslow, Macclesfield & Congleton (GR 856574)

How to get there

The village of Mow Cop is situated on a side road about 3 miles to the south of Congleton between the A34 to the west and A527 to the east. Follow signs to it from either main road. **Parking:** Free National Trust car park by Mow Cop Castle.

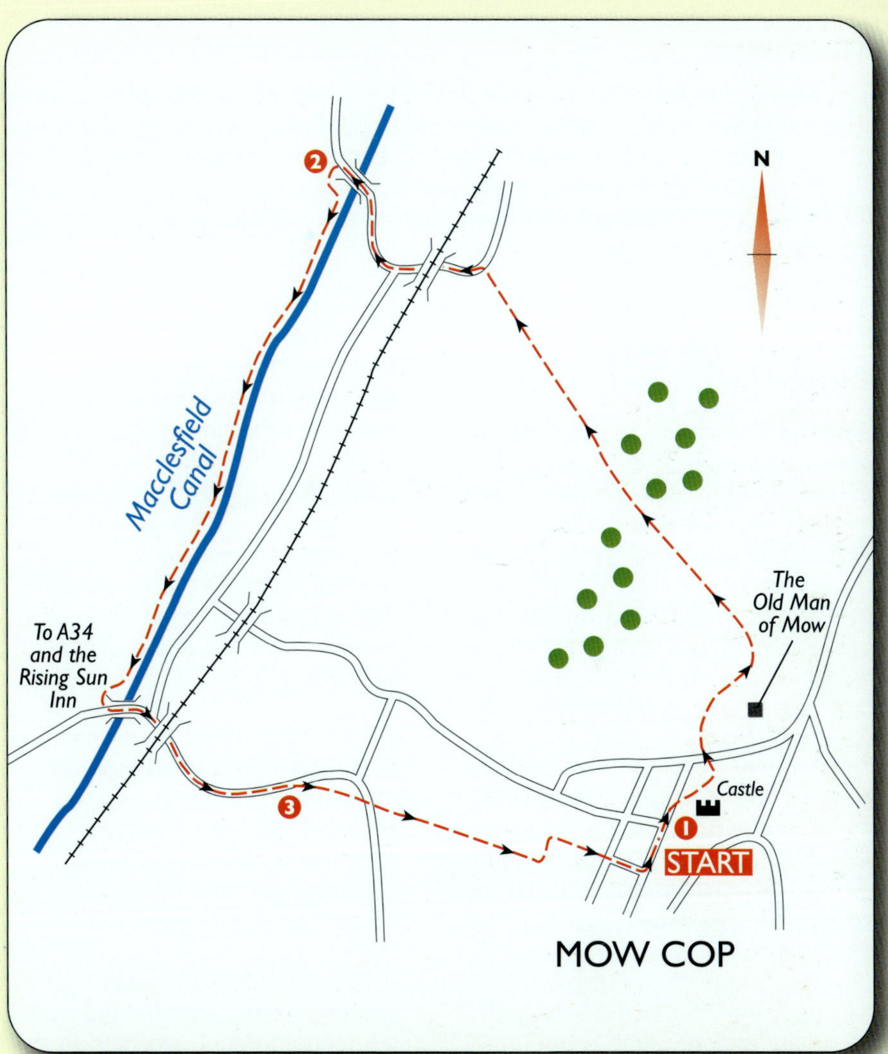

Introduction

From the grand vantage point of Mow Cop Castle, there are superb and extensive views looking westwards over the Cheshire plain as you descend from the ridge, across fields and through woodland, to the Macclesfield Canal. After a pleasant stroll along the towpath, you regain the ridge and walk through the small hilltop village before returning to the start.

Refreshments

The **Rising Sun Inn**, situated near where the route leaves the canal, offers a wide choice of light lunches (sandwiches, baguettes and jacket potatoes), roasts, grills, fish and vegetarian meals. There is a separate dining room, outside seating for fine weather and, as at many pubs in Cheshire, an open fire to sit by on cold days. Note that lunches are not served on Monday and Tuesday. Telephone: 01782 776235.

THE WALK

Although the hilltop ruin is called Mow Cop Castle, it is not a castle at all but an 18th-century folly. It was erected in 1754 by Randle Wilbraham of nearby Rode Hall as a summer house for his family and was built to resemble a ruined castle because he thought it would improve the view from the hall. It is now owned and maintained by the National Trust.

A stone at the base of the 'castle' records that it was near here that the Primitive Methodist movement was born. It arose out of an open-air meeting held at Mow Cop in the summer of 1807 by Hugh Bourne and William Clowes. On entering the village near the end of the walk you pass the Primitive Methodist Memorial chapel, built in the 1850s but extensively rebuilt in 1882 after severe storm damage. More details on Primitive Methodism can be found in Walk 18 which passes a museum to the movement in the village of Englesea-brook, around 20 miles away.

In the car park follow the **Gritstone Trail** sign towards the ruin and at the next sign, turn left along a path through heather. Bear left on joining a track to emerge onto a road, turn right and almost immediately turn left along a track. The track bends first left and then right and passes to the left of the **Old Man of Mow**.

The Old Man of Mow is almost as striking a hilltop monument as the mock castle. It is a rock pinnacle left after quarrying activities on the hill and from certain angles the shape resembles that of a giant man.

At a **South Cheshire Way** sign where the track bends right, turn left along an enclosed path to a stile. Climb it, walk along the left edge of the next two fields and in the corner of the second one, climb a stile to enter woodland. Head downhill through the trees, climb a stile at the bottom end and bear right to continue down by the right edge of a field. Keep

The ruins of the mock castle

ahead through a group of trees to enter the next field, continue along its right edge to a hedge corner and head down to a gate in the bottom right-hand field corner. Go through, walk down a track, bear left on joining a wide tree-lined track and continue down to a T-junction. Turn right along an enclosed track which bends left and heads down to a tarmac track. Keep along it and at a South Cheshire Way sign, turn left through a kissing gate and walk along a concrete path which bends right and passes under a railway bridge. Go through another kissing gate onto a lane, turn left and at a T-junction, turn right along **New Road** to the bridge over the **Macclesfield Canal**.

 ②

Cross the bridge, immediately turn sharp right down steps beside it to the towpath and turn right to go under the bridge.

The Macclesfield Canal was one of the last to be built, begun in 1826 and opened in 1831 just as the competition from the railways was starting. It runs from the Peak Forest Canal at Marple Junction to Kidsgrove where it joins the Trent and Mersey Canal and was constructed to provide a link between Manchester, the Potteries and the Black Country, as well as to serve the various industries around Macclesfield and Congleton. About ½ mile after joining the towpath, you pass some ornamental railings bordering the canal on the right instead of the usual hedge. Opposite these on the other side of the canal you see the façade of Ramsdell Hall, a fine Georgian mansion, in front of which manicured lawns sweep down to the canal. The railings were built by the Canal Company as part of an agreement between the company and the owner; the company acquired the most convenient route for the canal and in return the owner of the hall was compensated by having his glorious and unimpeded view across the Cheshire plain to the hills of North Wales preserved. After falling into a sorry state, the railings are currently being restored.

Walk beside the canal for 1 mile as far as **Bridge 87**. Just before reaching the bridge, turn right over a stile in a hedge and turn left up to a road. The Rising Sun Inn is a short distance to the right; the route continues to the left. Pass over the canal bridge and under a railway bridge and continue uphill for about ½ mile.

 ③

At a **Gritstone Way** sign, bear right along a straight, enclosed track (**Meadowside Lane**) which heads up to a road. Cross over, continue along the track opposite (The Brake) and where it bends right, keep ahead up an enclosed path. Climb a stile, walk uphill along the right edge of a field and, after the next stile, the way continues along an enclosed path. Pass between posts, turn left along an enclosed track and, at the corner of a wood, turn right onto a narrow path. Ascend steps, go through a gate and continue up an enclosed path which emerges onto a road in **Mow Cop village**. The Primitive Methodist Chapel is just to the left. Cross the road, keep ahead to a T-junction by the village shop and post office and turn left along **High Street.** The road leads back to the car park.

PLACE OF INTEREST NEARBY

The National Trust property of **Little Moreton Hall** lies just off the A34 about 3 miles south of Congleton. With its higgledy-piggledy appearance, overhanging upper storey and moat, this picturesque, half-timbered, 15th- and 16th-century manor house is a favourite subject for calendars and greetings cards. Telephone: 01260 272018.

12 Marbury Country Park and Great Budworth

The entrance to the country park

Distance 5 miles **Terrain** Easy walking by a lake, through woodlands and across fields, one modest climb and descent **Map** OS Explorer 267 Northwich & Delamere Forest (GR 652765)

How to get there

The entrance to Marbury Country Park is off the minor road through Anderton and Comberbach that links the A559 and the A533 to the north of Northwich. Follow the brown tourist signs from the main roads.
Parking: Pay car park at Marbury Country Park.

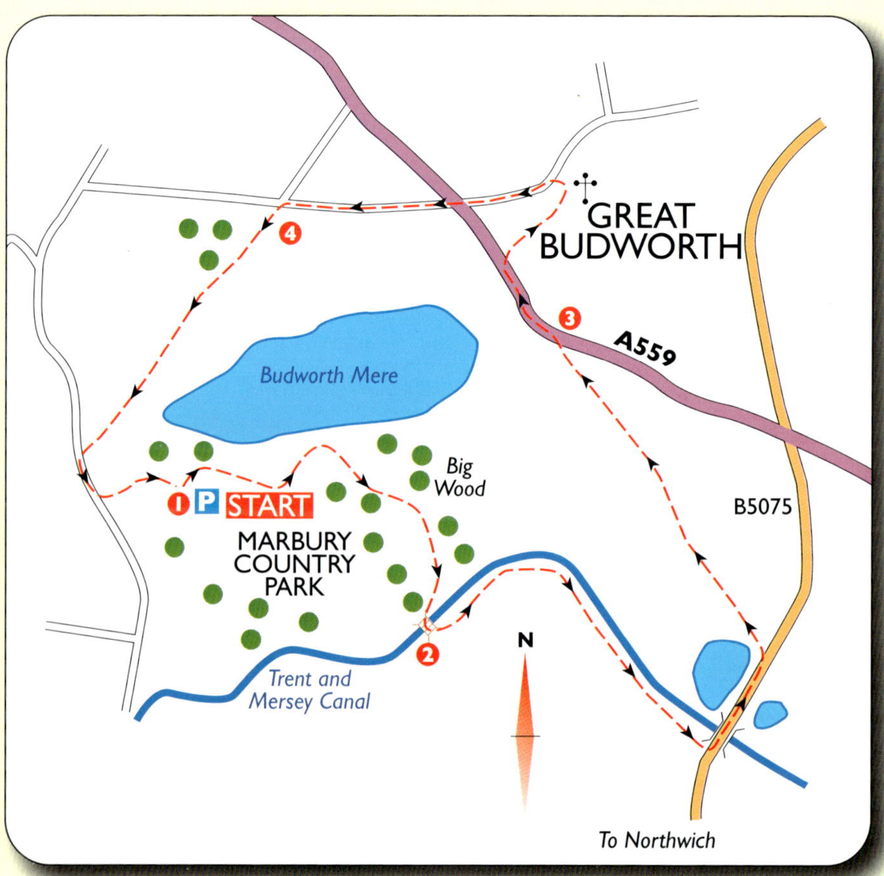

Introduction

The first part of the walk is beside Budworth Mere and through the lovely woodlands in Marbury Country Park. This is followed by a 1-mile stretch along the towpath of the Trent and Mersey Canal. Field paths lead up to the picturesque hill top village of Great Budworth and the final stretch is a gentle descent across fields, from which there are more attractive views across the mere.

Refreshments

The **George and Dragon** at Great Budworth is everyone's idea of a traditional English village pub. It is situated in one of the prettiest villages in Cheshire opposite the church and dates from the early 18th century. Inside it is welcoming and has lots of character, with old photographs on the walls in the comfortable seating areas. It provides a full range of cooked lunches, plus soup, sandwiches, salads and jacket potatoes as lighter alternatives. There is also a separate children's menu. Telephone: 01606 891317.

THE WALK

Marbury Country Park is part of the former estate of the Marbury family, who played an important part in the development of the salt industry around Northwich. The hall, built around 1850 in the style of a French chateau, was requisitioned in the Second World War and after damage and years of neglect, was demolished in 1959. The country park, created in 1975, is one of the most attractive in Cheshire and retains some of the grand avenues of lime trees planted by the Marburys.

Begin by going under an arch on the edge of the car park and walk along a path that passes to the right of an information board to a T-junction. Turn right along a straight tarmac track and, at a crossways by a fingerpost, turn left, following directions to **Mere** and **Big Wood**. At a fork on entering trees, take the right-hand path which curves right and heads down towards **Budworth Mere**. Keep ahead at a crossways and the path bends right through the trees alongside the mere. To the left are fine views across the water

with the tower of **Great Budworth church** prominent on the horizon. The path later moves away from the mere and continues through the trees to a fork by a fingerpost. Take the left-hand path, signposted to **Anderton Nature Park** and **Canal**, which winds through woodland to reach the canal. Turn right alongside it and turn left over a footbridge.

The Trent and Mersey Canal was built by James Brindley, the great 18th-century canal engineer. It was completed in 1777 and links the river Trent at Shardlow in Derbyshire with the river Mersey at Runcorn, a distance of 93 miles. Among its major sponsors were the pottery manufacturers of north Staffordshire, including Josiah Wedgwood.

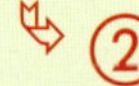

On the other side, turn left and walk along the towpath of the **Trent and Mersey Canal,** in the **Lion Salt Works** direction, to the first bridge (no 193). In front of the bridge, turn right up to the road – the Lion Salt Works is just to the right – and turn left to cross the canal bridge. Continue along the road – on both

sides there are pools or 'flashes' caused by salt mining subsidence – and at a public footpath sign, turn left along a tarmac track. Turn right through a kissing gate, continue in the same direction along the left edge of a field, go through another kissing gate and keep along the right edge of the next field. In the corner turn right over a stile, bear left and head diagonally across a field to a stile. Climb it and walk along the left edge of the next field to emerge onto a track. Cross it, walk along the right edge of two fields and climb a stile onto the road.

 ③

Turn left and at a public footpath sign, turn right through a kissing gate and head uphill across a field to its top edge. Turn right along the edge, go through a gate and walk along first a hedge-lined grassy track and later a tarmac drive towards **Great Budworth church**. Turn left, passing to the left of the church, to emerge onto the village street.

Great Budworth is an exceptionally pretty village with a number of half-timbered cottages lining its main street. Its large and handsome sandstone church, mainly built in the 15th century, is one of the finest in a county of grand churches. The long nave of six bays is most impressive and the tall west tower is a prominent landmark throughout much of the walk. The attractive old building on the north side of the churchyard is the former schoolroom.

Turn left down the street to a crossroads and keep ahead along **Budworth Lane**.

At a public footpath sign after ½ mile and opposite the road to Budworth Heath, turn left along a path through woodland. Go through a kissing gate on the edge of the trees and keep ahead across a field, later by a fence on the right, to a kissing gate. Go through, keep ahead to cross a footbridge over a brook, head up to a fence corner and continue along the right field edge to a kissing gate. After going through it, maintain the same direction across the next field and climb one more kissing gate onto a road. Turn left and at a **Marbury Country Park** sign turn left again along a tarmac drive. Take the first turning on the left to return to the start.

PLACE OF INTEREST NEARBY

The **Anderton Boat Lift** is one of the great wonders of the Industrial Revolution. It was built in the 1870s as an ingenious way to solve the problem of how to transfer boats from the Trent and Mersey Canal to the river Weaver below. It has recently been restored and you can take a ride on it and discover all about its history and construction in the visitor centre where there is a shop and café. The entrance is off the same road as the entrance to Marbury Country Park about ½ mile further south. Telephone: 01606 786777.

13 Little Budworth Country Park

A 'Christmas card' scene at Little Budworth Country Park

Distance 3½ miles **Terrain** A gently undulating route, mostly on woodland tracks and field paths **Map** OS Explorer 267 Northwich & Delamere Forest (GR 590655)

How to get there

From the A49 just to the south of its junction with the A54, turn along Coach Road (signposted to Little Budworth and Oulton Park) and after 1¼ miles you reach the car park on the left. **Parking:** Free car park at Little Budworth Country Park.

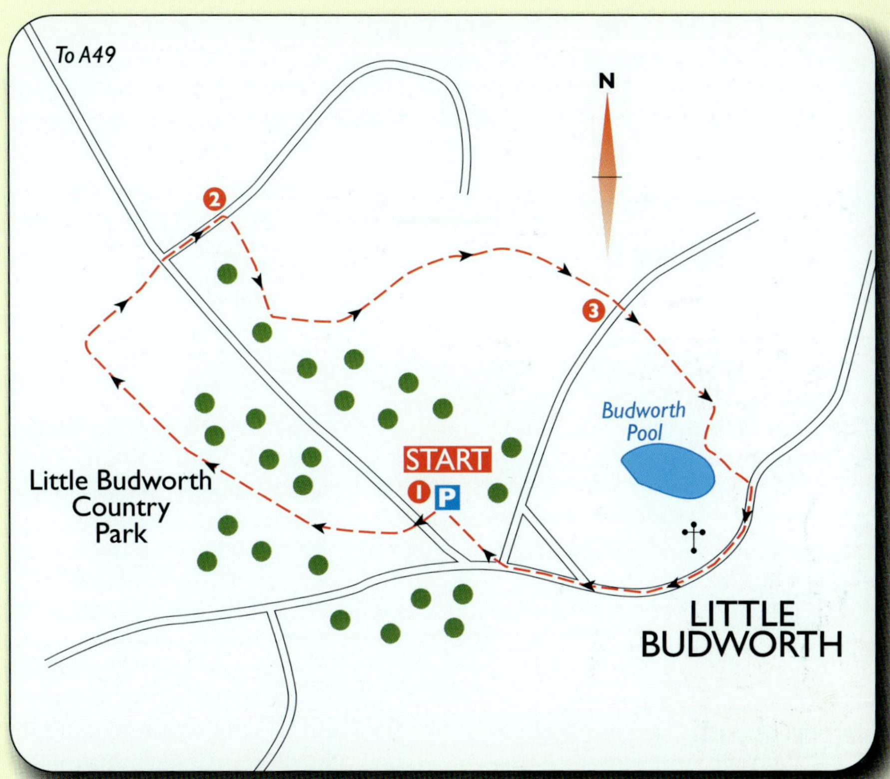

Introduction

Little Budworth Country Park only covers a small area but this delightful expanse of woodland, heath and pools is ideal for a pleasant and relaxing stroll at any time of the year. Possibly the highlight comes near the end of the walk where you can enjoy a particularly memorable view across Budworth Pool to the tower of the church at Little Budworth. Although this is generally a peaceful and tranquil walk, Oulton Park Racing Circuit is close by and therefore you will have to expect some noise on days when there is a race meeting.

Refreshments

The **Red Lion** in the centre of Little Budworth has been dispensing hospitality since 1797. This comfortable and cosy old pub – there are open fires – is open from 12 noon to 2 pm and from 6 pm onwards Monday to Saturday and all day on Sunday. There is an extensive choice of cooked meals (traditional roasts, grills, fish dishes) and lighter options (sandwiches, baguettes, omelettes, jacket potatoes) although only full lunches are available on Sunday. All dishes are made to order, using local produce where possible. In addition there is an attractive beer garden and bowling green. Telephone: 01829 760275.

THE WALK

Little Budworth Country Park is based on Little Budworth Common, a remnant of the ancient forests of Mara and Mondrum which once covered a huge swathe of northern and central Cheshire. Although predominantly woodland, it is also a rare example of lowland heath in this part of the country and contains several pools and wetland areas.

Start by crossing the road and taking the path opposite into woodland. Almost immediately turn right at a T-junction and, at a fork just ahead, take the left-hand path across a more open area before plunging into thick woodland again. Keep on the main path all the while, later picking up some yellow-waymarked posts. Look out for a crossways where a waymark directs you to turn left off the main path onto a narrower path. The path curves right and continues through the woodland, passing two waymarked posts before emerging from the trees, via a fence gap, onto a track. Turn right and, at a crossways, turn right again along

another track – signposted as a Restricted Byway – to a lane. Cross over and continue along the lane opposite (**Beech Road**).

At a public footpath sign to **White Hall Lane** and **Coach Road**, turn right onto a track by the left edge of woodland. After passing a house on the left, the track narrows to a path and heads gently down into the trees to a stile. Climb it, keep ahead, passing a pool on the right, and continue up to a fork. Take the left-hand, purple-waymarked path and almost immediately turn left onto a path that bears right and keeps parallel to the left edge of the woodland. On emerging from the trees, keep ahead along a track and, after passing a house on the left, the track heads gently downhill, passing to the right of a pool, to a crossways. Turn right beside a stream, climb a stile and immediately turn left and make for another stile in a fence. After climbing it, turn right and keep above the wooded valley parallel to the right field edge. Follow the edge to the left to a stile in the field corner, climb it and walk along an enclosed path. In front of a gate, turn right over another stile and head in a straight line across a field, making for a footpath post and stile on the far side to the left of farm buildings where you climb the stile onto a lane.

 ③

Turn left and at a Restricted Byway sign, turn right along a broad enclosed track. The route continues along a narrower enclosed path and at a public footpath sign to **Budworth Mere**, turn right over a stile. Walk across two fields and after climbing a stile at the end of the second field, turn left along a path beside **Budworth Pool**. To the right is a lovely view across the water to the tower of **Little Budworth church**. Climb a stile onto a lane and follow it into the village.

The small village of Little Budworth originated as a clearing in the thick forest that once covered much of this area. The church was mostly

Budworth pool

rebuilt around 1790 and only the early 16th-century west tower survives from the earlier structure.

The lane curves right by the church, passing the **Red Lion** and later the **Egerton Arms**. Continue along it and just beyond the east entrance to **Oulton Park**, a path on the right leads through the trees back to the start.

PLACE OF INTEREST NEARBY

Oulton Park has been a major racing circuit, staging championships for both cars and motorbikes since the 1950s. It developed out of the grounds of Oulton Hall, which was destroyed by fire in 1926, and is widely regarded as one of the most picturesque circuits in the country. It is close to Little Budworth and is signed from the A49 and A54. Telephone: 01829 760301.

14 | The Fringes of Delamere Forest

In the forest

How to get there

The Forestry Commission car park at Gresty's Waste is on the south side of the A54, ½ mile to the east of Kelsall and ¼ mile to the west of its junction with the A556. Parking: Free car park at Gresty's Waste.

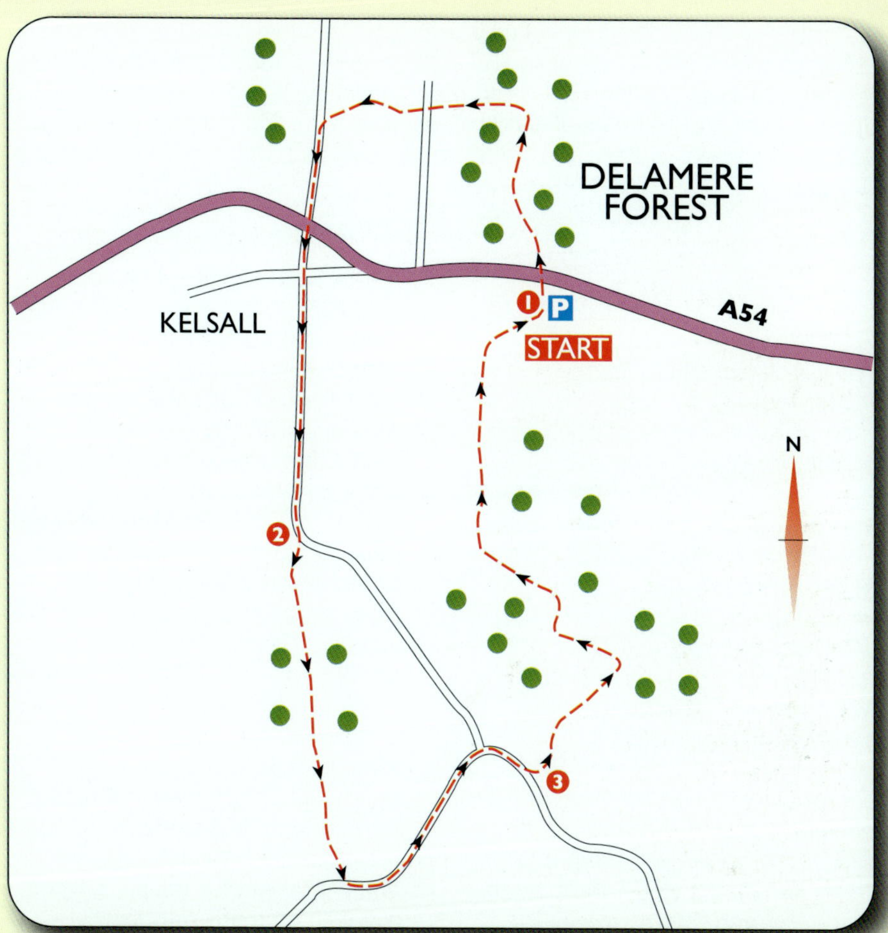

Introduction

The first and last parts of the walk are through wooded areas on the southern fringes of Delamere Forest. The remainder is across fields and through wooded valleys and from the higher points there are grand and extensive views across the surrounding countryside, especially looking westwards towards the hills of North Wales.

Refreshments

The **Summertrees Tea Room**, conveniently situated about two-thirds of the way around the walk, immediately impresses visitors with the sign by the entrance which states that dogs and walkers with muddy boots are welcome. It is an ideal spot to stop for a morning coffee, light lunch or afternoon tea and provides a wide range of sandwiches, salads, jacket potatoes, hot snacks and homemade cakes and pies in a pleasant and informal setting. Telephone: 01829 751145.

THE WALK

The 2,400 acres of Delamere Forest represent a fragment of the vast adjacent forests of Mara and Mondrum which in the Middle Ages extended over much of northern and central Cheshire between the river Mersey and Nantwich. These forests were originally the hunting ground of the powerful earls of Chester but became a royal possession in the 14th century when Edward III acquired the earldom. Extensive felling, especially in the 17th and 18th centuries, reduced the forest to its present size and it mainly comprises conifer plantations with some deciduous woodlands, open grassland and meres. It was the meres that gave this forested area its alternative and present name: the Forest of the Meres or de la mer.

Gresty's Waste was a toll point on a turnpike road through the forest. The present A54 is roughly on the line of that road.

Start by taking the **Sandstone Trail** along a path through trees parallel to the A54 and at a fingerpost, turn right to cross the busy main road. Continue along the track ahead going gently uphill through the forest and at a Sandstone Trail footpath sign turn left in the **Yeld Lane** direction. After passing a barrier, keep ahead along a lane to a T-junction, turn left and head gently downhill along **Yeld Lane**. Cross a bridge over the A54, to reach a crossroads on the edge of **Kelsall** and continue uphill.

After ½ mile where the lane bends left, keep ahead along a tarmac track but almost immediately bear right across grass in front of a house, passing a public footpath sign to Willington, and keep along the right inside edge of woodland to a kissing gate. Go through, walk along the left edge of the next three fields and, in the corner of the third one, go through a kissing gate and bear left to descend a flight of steps. The path curves right, descends more steps and continues below steeply sloping woodland on the left.

This is a most attractive part of the walk. The wooded valley has a secluded and genuinely remote feel and the views ahead, looking across Cheshire to the Welsh hills are superb.

After reaching the bottom of the slope, continue along a track to a lane. Turn left uphill along the winding lane to a T-junction and turn right along **Tirley Lane**.

The route near Kelsall

 ③

Where the lane bends right, turn left over a stile – here rejoining the **Sandstone Trail** – and walk along an enclosed path beside the **Summertrees Tea Room**. Go through a kissing gate, walk along a right field edge and, just before reaching the corner, look out for where you turn right through another kissing gate. Turn left, head downhill along the left field edge and in the bottom corner, go through a kissing gate, descend steps and turn left to re-enter the forest. Head gently downhill, turn right at a **Sandstone Trail** post and at a T-junction, turn left along a well-surfaced track. Where this track bends left, continue uphill along a sandy track to a T-junction. Turn right along a path – following the regular **Sandstone Trail** signs – climb two stiles in quick succession, keep ahead, negotiate another pair of stiles and the path bends right and heads quite steeply downhill through woodland to a footbridge. Cross it, climb a flight of steps and, at the top, turn right to return to the car park.

PLACE OF INTEREST NEARBY

The remains of **Beeston Castle**, built in the 13th century as a defence against Welsh raids, sprawl over a dramatic cliff top that rises abruptly from the Cheshire plain. The climb up to the top is well worth the effort for the magnificent all round views that extend from the line of the Peak District moorlands in the east to the hills of North Wales in the west. The castle is signposted from the A49 about 2 miles south of Tarporley. Telephone: 01829 260464.

15 Dee Valley between Farndon and Churton

The river Dee

Distance 5 miles **Terrain** An entirely flat walk mostly across fields and riverside meadows **Map** OS Explorer 257 Crewe & Nantwich (GR 413544)

How to get there

Farndon lies on the north bank of the river Dee approximately 8 miles south of Chester and ½ mile north of the A534 Nantwich to Wrexham road. **Parking:** Free parking area at the picnic site by the bridge over the river.

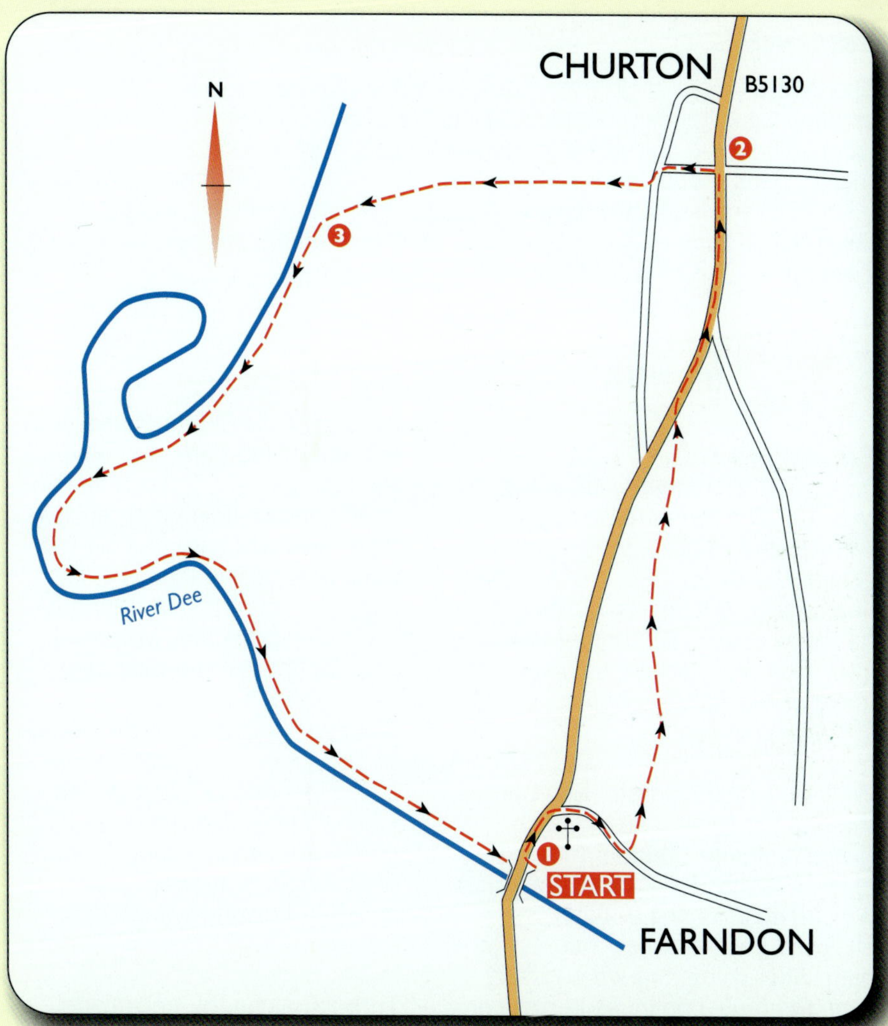

Introduction

The first part of the route takes you northwards across fields and along a road from Farndon to the nearby village of Churton. You then turn westwards to follow a track down to the banks of the river Dee which here forms the border between England and Wales. The final part of the walk is a lovely stroll mostly beside the river across a series of lush meadows interspersed with small areas of woodland.

Refreshments

The **White Horse** at Churton, situated at the crossroads in the centre of this small village, has both a spacious interior and a comprehensive menu. The latter includes a full range of cooked meals and a good choice of lighter meals, plus soup and sandwiches. There is a pleasant conservatory restaurant and attractive outside areas to make use of in fine weather. Meals are served both at lunchtime and in the evening, except on Monday. Telephone: 01829 270208.

THE WALK

Farndon is a border village, occupying sandstone cliffs above the river Dee here crossed by a picturesque bridge. On the opposite side of the river is the Welsh village of Holt with the sparse remains of a medieval castle. The bridge dates from the 14th century as does the tower of the nearby church.

Walk up to the road and turn right through the village. At a public footpath sign to Churton, turn left along a tarmac track (**Walkers Lane**) which becomes first a rough enclosed track and later narrows to a path. After going through a kissing gate, the route continues in more or less a straight line, sometimes across fields and sometimes along the field edges, passing through a succession of kissing gates. Finally veer slightly left across the last in the series of fields and go through a kissing gate onto a road. Turn right and follow it for ½ mile into **Churton** – there is a pavement on the left.

In front of the **White Horse**, turn left along **Hob Lane** and where the lane bends left, keep ahead gently downhill along an enclosed track (**Knowl Lane**). Follow the track around two right and left bends to reach a stile. Climb it, keep ahead to enter woodland and continue to the **river Dee**.

The river Dee rises on the slopes of Snowdonia and flows through Bala Lake and on through the Vale of Llangollen before turning northwards and forming for part of its length a natural border between England and Wales.

Turn left along the tree-lined riverbank and after going through a kissing gate, continue along the right edge of a meadow. Go through a kissing gate, keep ahead through a small belt of trees, go through another gate and continue across the next meadow. At the corner of the meadow where the river bends

Farndon Bridge

sharply to the right, go through a kissing gate, cross a track, go through another kissing gate and continue along the left edge of a meadow to a public footpath sign. Turn left through a gate, go through another one and, at a crossways of tracks, turn right beside pools on the left. Look out for where a waymarked post directs you to turn right up steps onto a path which bends left and continues to a kissing gate. Go through, continue across two meadows, with an intervening belt of trees and, in the corner of the second meadow, follow its edge to the left and turn right through a kissing gate. The route continues by the river across more meadows and through more kissing gates to **Farndon Bridge**. Go under an arch of the bridge to return to the start.

PLACE OF INTEREST NEARBY

Erdigg, a fine 18th-century country house just across the Welsh border. There is plenty to interest the whole family with a rare 18th-century garden, extensive parkland, restaurant and horse-drawn carriage rides. It is situated about 2 miles south of Wrexham and is signposted from the A483 and A525. Telephone: 01978 315151.

16 Bulkeley Hill Wood and Raw Head

The wooded sandstone ridge near Higher Burwardsley

Distance 5½ miles **Terrain** Clear and well-signed paths over hills, through woodland and across fields, with several fairly modest climbs
Map OS Explorer 257 Crewe & Nantwich (GR 523565)

How to get there

Follow signs to Higher Burwardsley, and brown tourist signs to Cheshire (or Candle) Workshops, from the A49 near Bunbury and Beeston. **Parking:** Free parking at the front part of the car park at the Cheshire Workshops at Higher Burwardsley.

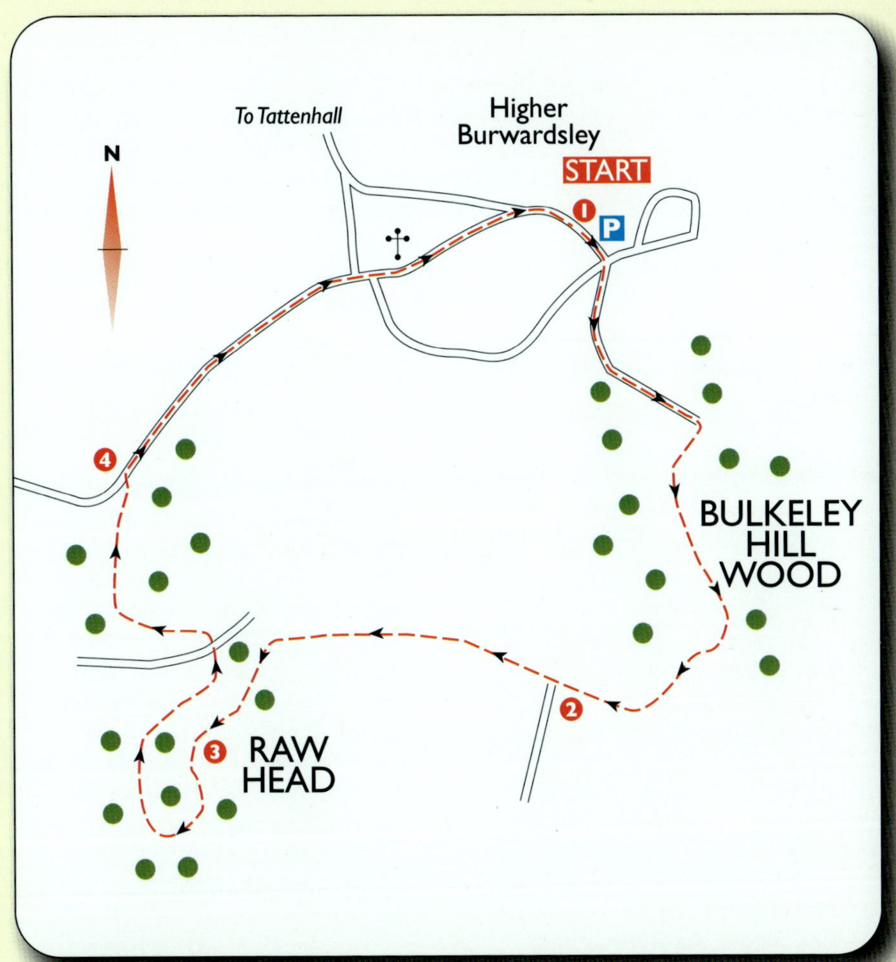

Introduction

Much of this walk is along the well-wooded sandstone ridge that runs across Cheshire and it includes two climbs. The first and steeper one is to the top of Bulkeley Hill Wood and the second, more gradual ascent is to the highest point on the Sandstone Trail, the 746-ft high Raw Head. The woodland walking is exceptionally attractive and from the two summits, and indeed for much of this route, the views over the Cheshire plain are magnificent, extending to the line of the Peak District hills, the distant industries of Merseyside and the mountains of North Wales.

Refreshments

There is a choice at Higher Burwardsley between the Pheasant Inn and the restaurant at Cheshire Workshops. The **Pheasant Inn** occupies an enviable situation with superb views over the Cheshire plain from its attractive outside seating areas. It is no less attractive inside and offers a wide range of mouth-watering full and lighter meals in comfortable surroundings. Telephone: 01829 770434.

If you prefer somewhat simpler food at lower prices, the self-service restaurant just across the road at **Cheshire Workshops** is a good alternative. Again there are both cooked meals and lighter options and you still get the views. It is open every day from 10 am to 5 pm. Telephone: 01829 770401.

THE WALK

At the Cheshire Workshops – alternatively called the Candle Workshops – you can watch skilled craftsmen practising the ancient craft of candle making and even have a go yourself. There is a shop selling a wide range of gifts, a restaurant and plenty of activities for children. Telephone: 01829 770401.

Start by taking the narrow lane opposite the car park entrance which curves right to a crossroads. Turn right along a lane, follow it around a left bend and head uphill. Where the lane peters out, turn right onto a track, here joining the **Sandstone Trail**, signposted to **Bulkeley Hill** and **Raw Head**. Look out for where a Sandstone Trail waymark directs you to turn left up steps – there is a National Trust sign for **Bulkeley Hill Wood** here – and head uphill through the trees to the top of the wooded hill. Continue along a winding, ridge top path, following regular Sandstone Trail signs, and after passing through a hedge gap, where you leave **Bulkeley Hill Wood**, the path curves right and descends to a kissing gate on the edge of the trees. Go through, bear slightly right and walk across a field to emerge onto a lane (**Coppermines Lane**).

Cross it, keep ahead along a track and where it bears left, continue along a tree-lined path. Look out for where a Sandstone Trail waymark directs you to turn left through a kissing gate and continue along an enclosed track. Gaps in the trees on the right reveal grand views over the Cheshire countryside. From one of these gaps – where there is a

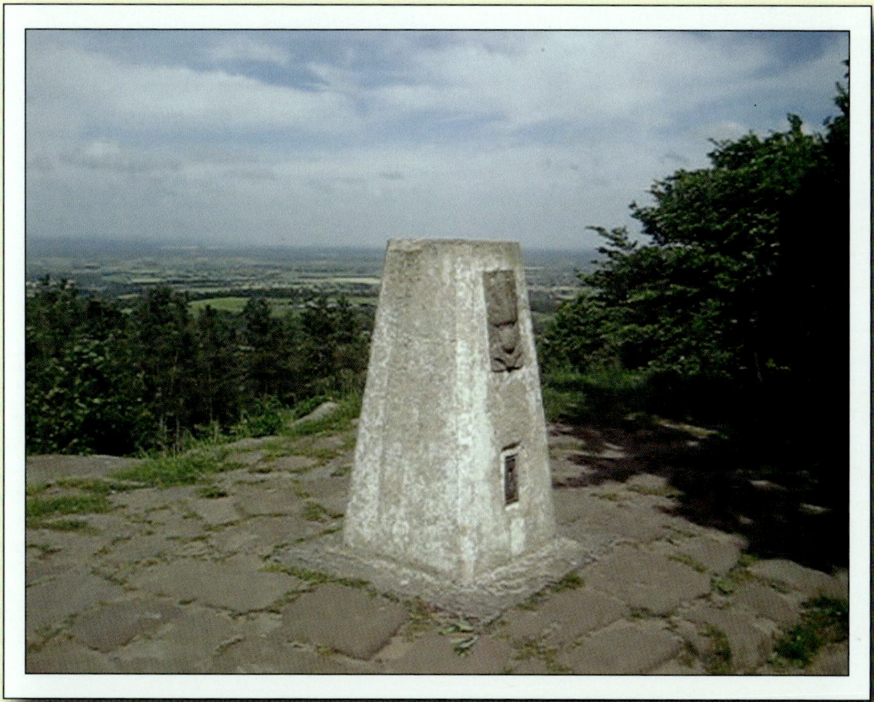

The view from the summit of Raw Head

thoughtfully provided bench – there is a particularly outstanding view that includes **Beeston and Peckforton castles** on their twin wooded hills and,
in the far distance the **tower of Liverpool Cathedral** is visible on clear days. The path later climbs, via steps in places, and continues by a wire fence on the left, twisting and turning and passing several rocky outcrops, to reach the trig point on the summit of **Raw Head**.

At 746 ft, Raw Head is the highest point on the Sandstone Trail. Despite this relatively modest height, the extensive panoramic views from here, over wooded hillsides and ridges and across the flatter terrain of the Cheshire plain, are magnificent.

③

Bear left past the trig point to continue along the ridge-top path which bends right and descends a flight of steps. Keep ahead, follow the path around a left bend and turn right at a waymarked post, here leaving the Sandstone Trail. Head down through the trees and, at the next waymarked post, turn sharp right and descend a long flight of steps to reach a track at a U-bend. Bear right along the track which contours along the face of the thickly wooded hill and pass beside a gate onto a narrow lane. Cross over, take the downhill path opposite through a young plantation, cross a track and climb a stile. Bear slightly left across a field to a footpath post on the far side and continue past it into the trees to a stile. After climbing it, follow the path through **Bodnook Wood** and descend to a stile on the edge of the trees. Climb it, immediately turn right over another one and head downhill across a field to another stile. After climbing it, keep along the right field edge, heading down into a dip and up again, and in the field corner climb a stile onto a road.

Keep ahead and after just over ½ mile, turn right into Church Road. Head uphill, follow the road around a left bend, passing to the right of Burwardsley church, and continue along a lane to a T-junction. Turn right and head uphill to a crossroads. The Pheasant Inn is to the left and a right turn along Barracks Lane returns you to the start.

PLACE OF INTEREST NEARBY

Bunbury Watermill, built around the middle of the 19th century, is located just to the east of the village of Bunbury and has been restored after ceasing production in 1960. After a tour of the mill, visitors can purchase some of the wholemeal flour produced there. The mill is accessed from the A49 and A51 but is only open from April to the end of September on Sundays and Bank Holiday Mondays between 1 pm and 4 pm. Telephone: 01829 261422.

17 Nantwich and the Weaver Valley

Nantwich town centre

Distance 4 miles **Terrain** Flat walking by a river, across fields, along a canal towpath and a final stretch along a road **Map** OS Explorer 257 Crewe & Nantwich (GR 652524)

How to get there

Nantwich is situated 4 miles to the south of Crewe, 17 miles to the west of Stoke-on-Trent and about 8 miles from junction 16 of the M6. **Parking:** Plenty of pay car parks at Nantwich.

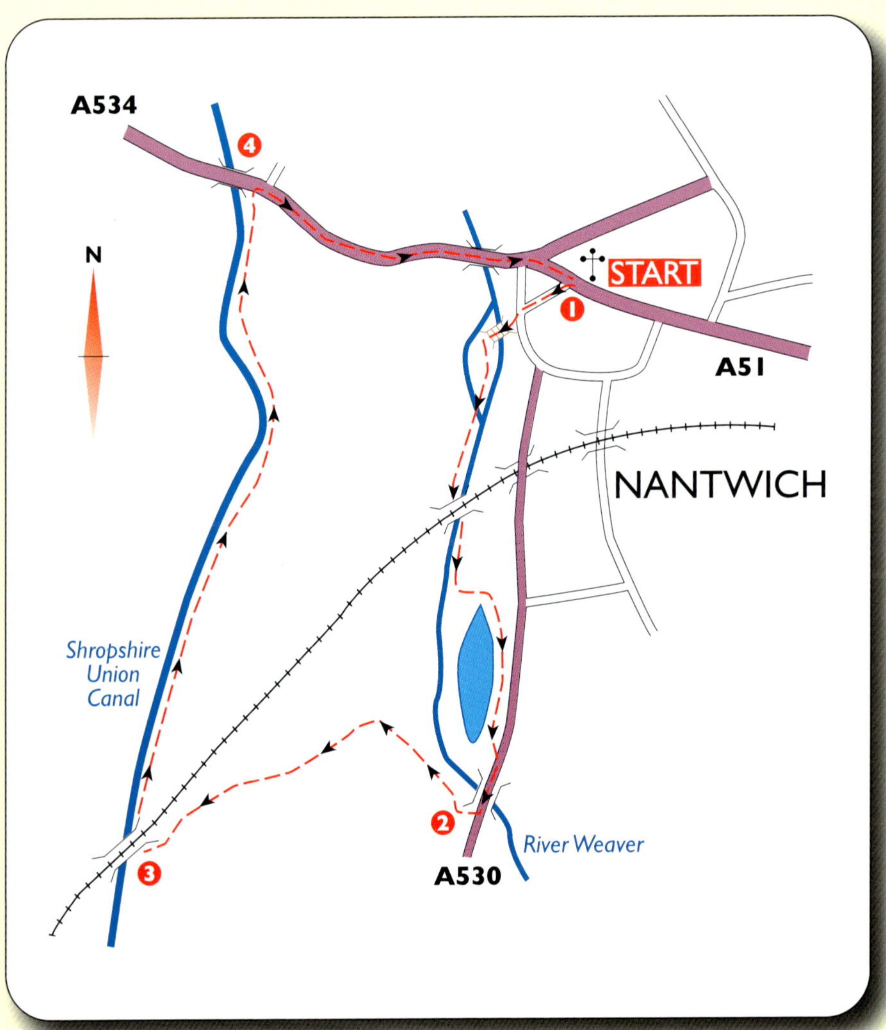

Introduction

This is very much a waterside walk. The first part is by the river Weaver, the last section is along the towpath of the Shropshire Union Canal and the two waterways are linked by field paths on the outward stretch and a road on the final leg. There are wide views across predominantly flat countryside and there is plenty to explore in Nantwich, an exceptionally attractive and interesting old town.

Refreshments

Nantwich is full of pubs, restaurants and teashops. If you want to choose a place that combines good food with lots of character and atmosphere, you could do no better than the **Nantwich Bookshop Coffee Lounge**. It is conveniently situated at the start of the walk and housed in two black and white Elizabethan buildings built in the late 1580s following the Great Fire of 1583. The ground floor is the bookshop and the first floor is the coffee lounge. It is open Monday to Saturday from 9 am to 4.30 pm and serves morning coffee and afternoon tea as well as a variety of light lunches that include sandwiches, salads, jacket potatoes and baguettes. There are two rooms and in one of them you can relax in armchairs and sofas. Telephone: 01270 611665.

THE WALK

The size and splendour of the church indicates that, in the Middle Ages, Nantwich was a town of considerable prosperity. The basis of its wealth was the production of salt; the place name ending 'wich' means salt, as in the nearby towns of Northwich and Middlewich, as well as Droitwich in Worcestershire. During its long history Nantwich has suffered several disasters. It was burnt down by the Normans in the late 11th century and was regularly subjected to attacks from across the Welsh border but the major calamity occurred in 1583 when most of the town was destroyed by a fire which raged for 20 days. Rebuilding commenced soon afterwards and some of the timber used was donated by Elizabeth I from the nearby Royal Forest of Delamere. The majority of the black and white timber-framed buildings that are such an attractive feature of the town centre date from this late 16th-century rebuilding, including the picturesque Crown Hotel near the start of the walk. In addition Nantwich is graced by many dignified Georgian buildings.

Among the few buildings to survive the 'Great Fire' of 1583 is the magnificent cruciform church, appropriately described as 'the cathedral of south Cheshire' and widely acknowledged as one of the finest parish churches in England. It was built in the late 14th century and the dominant feature of the exterior is the unusual octagonal central tower. When walking around the spacious interior, look out for the intricately-carved 14th-century choir stalls in the vaulted chancel.

The walk begins in the town centre by the church and war memorial. With your back to the church, turn

left and take the first street on the right (**Mill Street**) which leads down to a main road. Cross over, keep ahead to cross a footbridge over an arm of the **river Weaver** and immediately turn left along a tarmac path beside the river. Cross a footbridge over the main channel of the river and keep ahead by the now reunited river to a crossways. Turn left and at a T-junction turn left over another footbridge and turn right to continue along the opposite bank of the Weaver, passing under a railway bridge. The path curves left and right, turns left again over another footbridge and continues by the river, later bending left across the end of a pool. Go through a gate into a car park and picnic area and turn right to walk across the grass, between a road on the left and the pool on the right. Continue along the road – there is a pavement on the left side – and cross a bridge over the river.

 ②

At a public bridleway sign, turn right through a gate and walk across a field to a gate on the far side. Go through, cross a footbridge over a stream and go through another gate. Bear right gently uphill across the next field, passing a waymarked post, to its right edge and bear left to keep by the edge to a gate. Go through and ahead are two gates. Go through the left-hand yellow-waymarked one, bear left and walk diagonally across a field to a stile in the far corner. Climb it, keep along the right edge of the next field but after a few yards, turn right over two stiles in quick succession and veer slightly left across the field, looking out for a stile on the far side. After climbing this double stile, continue in the same direction across the next field to the base of a railway embankment and bear left alongside it to a gate. Go through and head gently uphill along the right edge of the next field.

At the top turn right over a stile just in front of a canal bridge and descend steps to the towpath of the **Shropshire Union Canal**.

The Shropshire Union Canal was one of the many engineering triumphs of Thomas Telford. It was one of the last great canals of the Canal Age and was only completed in 1835, around the time when the development of the railways was sounding the death knell of the canals as commercial waterways. It runs for approximately 66 miles from the edge of Wolverhampton through Staffordshire, Shropshire and Cheshire to the river Mersey at Ellesmere Port.

Turn right, pass under a railway bridge and keep along the towpath for 1¼ miles into **Nantwich**. After crossing an aqueduct over a road, turn right and descend steps to the road.

Cross over at traffic lights and keep ahead along **Welsh Row**. Cross the bridge over the **river Weaver**, keep ahead into the town centre and turn right at a T-junction to return to the start.

PLACE OF INTEREST NEARBY

There is something for the whole family at **Stapeley Water Gardens**, which are off the A529 just to the south of Nantwich and are signposted from junction 16 of the M6. As well as the water gardens themselves, children can see rare and exotic tropical animals and plants in the rainforest surroundings of the Palms Tropical Oasis and there is everything for the home and garden in the huge garden centre. There is also an Italian garden, a café and one of the largest angling stores in the country. Telephone: 01270 623868.

18 Barthomley and Englesea-brook

Barthomley's fine medieval church

Distance 4 miles **Terrain** Mainly flat walking across fields and along lanes, with a few steep gullies; muddy and uneven ground in places
Map OS Explorer 257 Crewe & Nantwich (GR 767525)

How to get there

Barthomley is only 1¼ miles from junction 16 of the M6. From the junction take the B5078 towards Alsager and after ½ mile, turn left down the lane signposted to Barthomley. **Parking:** Careful roadside parking by the White Lion.

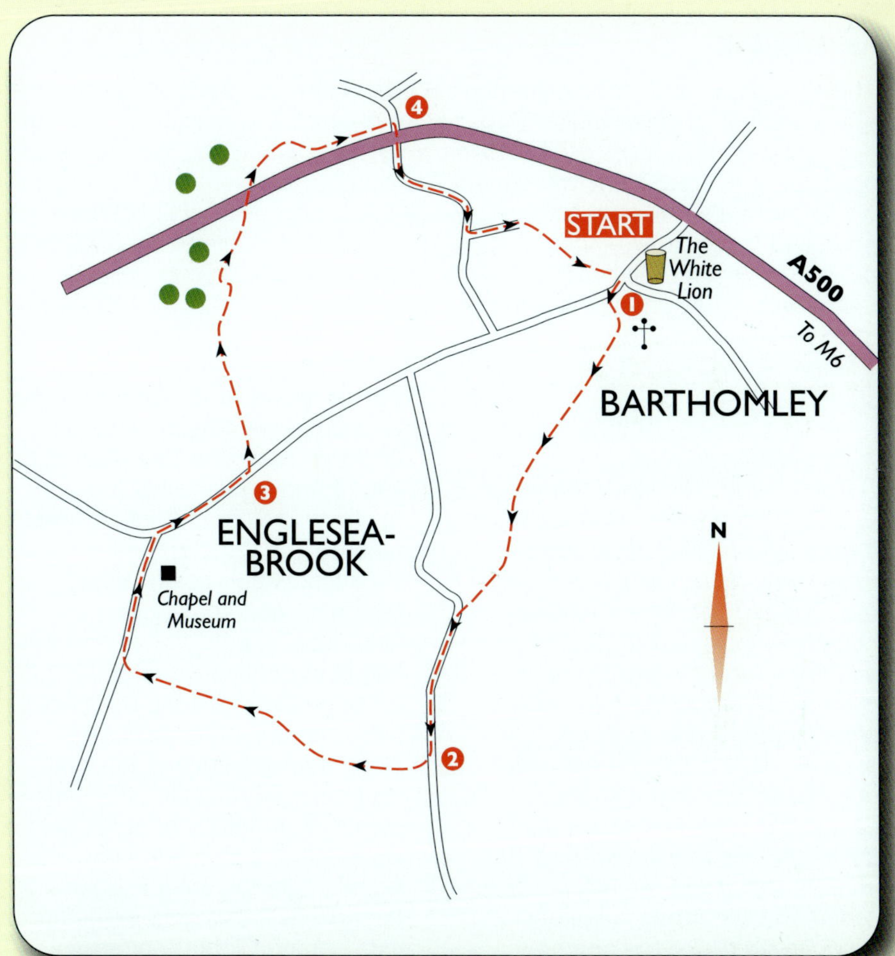

Introduction

The walk starts in the small, quiet village of Barthomley and takes you across lush fields and along lanes to the equally quiet village of Engleseabrook, noted for its early 19th-century Primitive Methodist chapel and museum. On the return leg to Barthomley you have to cross the busy A500 twice, although on the second occasion it is via a bridge. Throughout the walk there are wide views across the gently undulating countryside of south Cheshire. Note that there are over 30 stiles to negotiate and some of them require a fair degree of agility.

Refreshments

The thatched and timber-framed **White Lion** at Barthomley is the quintessential English village pub, full of character and with a cosy and welcoming atmosphere, especially on a cold day when you can sit by the open fires. It dates from the early 17th century and some of the original wattle and daub can still be seen. Meals are served every day between 12 noon and 2 pm. A wide variety of cooked lunches and lighter alternatives is provided, though whether 'light' is the appropriate adjective to describe the huge sandwiches on offer is another matter. Telephone: 01270 882242.

THE WALK

Despite being little more than ¾ mile from the M6, Barthomley is a quiet and tucked away sort of village with a surprisingly remote feel. The red sandstone medieval church is dedicated to St Bertoline, a little-known 8th-century saint. It is unusually imposing for a village church, with a fine 15th-century arcaded nave of almost cathedral-like proportions and a superb carved oak roof. The explanation for this is that for many centuries the church was at the hub of the Crewe estate and the family regularly provided funds for the church's enlargement and restoration. Several members of the Crewe and related families are buried here.

①

Start by the **White Lion** and walk along the lane signposted to Weston and Betley. Take the first track on the left (signposted to Village Hall), passing to the right of the church, and continue through the village hall car park. At the far end of the car park, keep ahead along an enclosed path to a stile, turn right over it and immediately turn left to climb another one into a field. Ignoring the Circular Walk waymark which points ahead, bear right and head across the field, looking out for a stile in the hedge in front. After climbing it, continue along the right edge of a field, climb another stile, bear left along the right edge of the next field and climb a stile by a hedge corner. Turn left along a left field edge, climb a stile and bear slightly right to continue across the next field to a stile in the far right corner. Climb it, cross a tarmac drive, climb another stile and continue across the corner of the next field to a stile. Climb it onto a lane and turn left.

 ②

After nearly ½ mile, turn right over a stile, at a public footpath sign, and walk along an enclosed path, between woodland on the left and the garden of a house on

The White Lion inn at Barthomley

the right, to another stile. After climbing it, the route continues across a succession of fields and over a series of stiles. In the third field, you make for the corner of a hedge and keep by the hedge to a stile. Climb it, bear right and continue in more or less the same direction across another succession of fields and over another series of stiles to emerge finally onto a road. Turn right through the hamlet of **Englesea-brook**, passing the **Primitive Methodist museum**, to a road junction and turn right, in the Barthomley direction.

The Primitive Methodist movement was founded at nearby Mow Cop (visited on Walk 11) on the Cheshire-Staffordshire border in 1807. It was a breakaway group whose members had become disillusioned with the mainstream Methodist church which they felt had moved too far way from the ideals of its founder John Wesley. The museum at Englesea-brook is housed in an early chapel, built in 1828, and contains many exhibits concerned with the history and development of the movement. In the burial ground opposite is a memorial to Hugh Bourne, one of its co-founders, who is buried here. For details of opening times phone 01270 820836.

 **③**

After just over ¼ mile turn left over a stile at a public footpath sign and walk across a field towards farm buildings making for a stile in the far right corner. Climb it, walk along an enclosed path, turn right over another stile and turn left along the left field edge. Climb two stiles in quick succession and keep ahead to climb another one. As you descend an embankment, there is a fine view ahead over the Cheshire countryside. At the bottom keep ahead across rough grass, looking out for a waymarked footbridge, cross it and turn left along the left edge of a field. Follow the field edge to the right – woodland over to the left – and follow the edge to the right again. Turn left over a stile and carefully cross the busy A500 to a public footpath sign and stile on the other side. After climbing the stile, turn right across an area of rough, sloping grass and curve right to head up a steep embankment to another stile. Climb it, bear left away from the field edge and descend another embankment to a footbridge. On the other side of the bridge the path forks; take the right-hand path and head up again to a pair of stiles in the top left corner of the field. Climb the left-hand one of the two stiles and walk along the right edge of the next two fields, climbing two stiles and keeping parallel to the A500. After climbing the second stile, turn left and climb another stile onto a lane.

 **④**

Turn right, cross a bridge over the A500, continue along the lane to a junction and turn left at a No Through Road sign along **Smithy Lane West**. Where the lane ends at a gate just beyond a farm, turn right over a stile and walk across a field. Climb a stile in the corner and continue along an enclosed path which widens into a track and continues down to a road in Barthomley. Turn right to the start.

PLACE OF INTEREST NEARBY

Bridgemere Garden World is one of the largest garden centres in the country. It has an enormous variety of plants for sale, as well as garden, patio and conservatory furniture, barbecues and much more. Visitors can also wander round over 20 display gardens and there is a restaurant. It lies off the A51 between Nantwich and Stone and is signposted from junctions 15 and 16 of the M6. Tel: 01270 521 100.

19 Audlem and the Shropshire Union Canal

The Shroppie Fly, Audlem

Distance 3 miles **Terrain** Flat walking across fields, through woodland and along a canal towpath **Map** OS Explorer 257 Crewe & Nantwich (GR 660436)

How to get there

Audlem is situated at the junction of the A525 and A529, about 7 miles south of Nantwich. **Parking:** Free car park at Audlem.

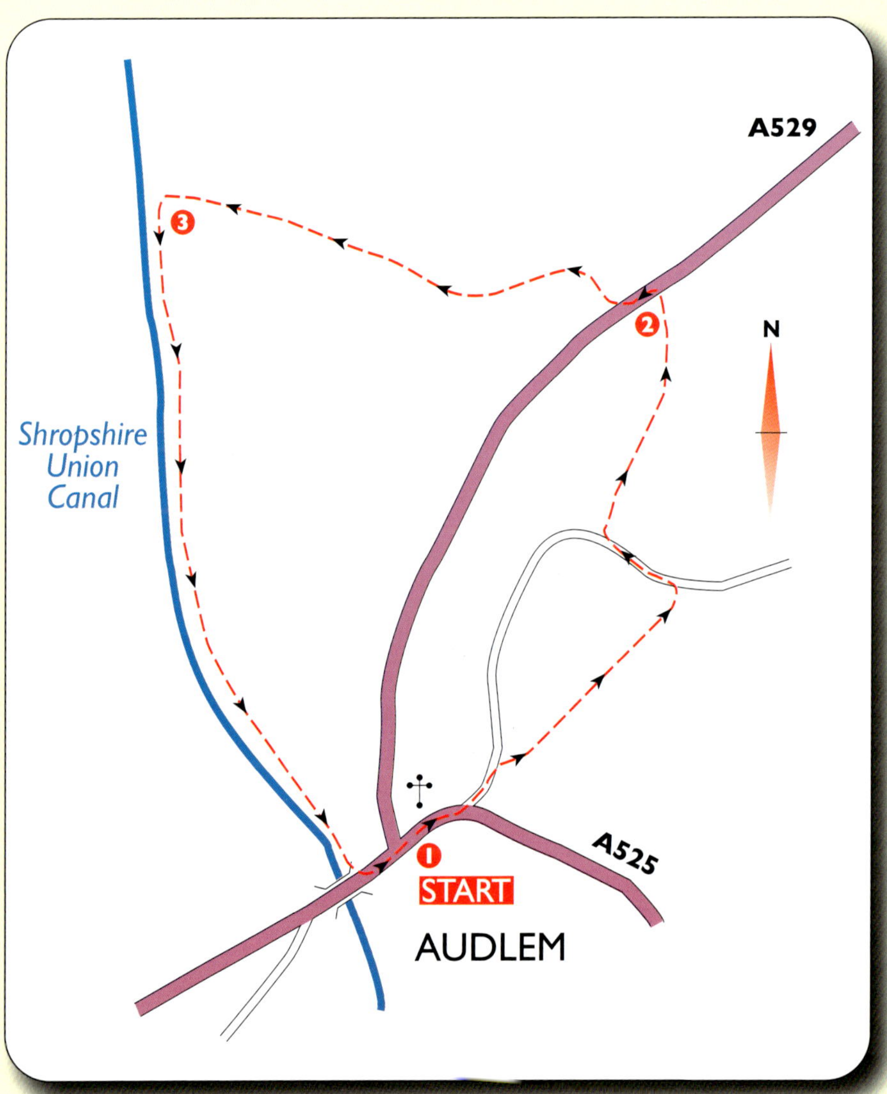

Introduction

The walk explores the pleasant and gentle countryside of the Weaver valley in south Cheshire to the north of the village of Audlem. There are wide views across fields, a secluded wooded valley and the final leg is along a particularly attractive and tranquil stretch of the Shropshire Union Canal.

Refreshments

There are pubs and cafés at Audlem. Towards the end of the walk you pass the **Shroppie Fly**, a traditional canalside pub. It was originally built as a canal warehouse and gets its name from the fly boats, faster and sleeker than the usual canal boats, which used to carry goods along the Shropshire Union Canal. Food is home-cooked and there is an extensive menu. Main meals include fish, grills and meat dishes and the pub also serves lighter meals (burgers and filled rolls) children's meals and a good choice of desserts. Make sure you have a huge appetite before you order any of the filled rolls! There is also a good selection of beers. In fine weather it is particularly pleasant to sit at the outside tables overlooking the canal. Telephone: 01270 811772.

THE WALK

Audlem is the most southerly village in Cheshire and lies close to the Shropshire and Staffordshire borders. It is situated in the Weaver valley on the east bank of the Shropshire Union Canal. On a knoll above The Square in the village centre stands the sturdy sandstone church. It dates from the 13th and 14th centuries and was extended and restored by the Victorians. Below the church is The Shambles, a 17th-century market cross.

Start in **The Square** and facing the church, turn right along **Stafford Street**. Follow the road around a right bend and at a crossroads opposite **School Lane**, turn left along a lane. Where the lane bends left, keep ahead along a track called **Mill Lane**. This hedge-lined track eventually bends left to emerge onto a lane. Turn left and at a public footpath sign where the lane bends left, turn right along a tarmac drive to **The Parkes**. Just before a pair of white gateposts, bear left off the drive to a kissing gate. Go through, walk along the left edge of a field, by a fence and line of trees on the left, and continue through a succession of gates to emerge onto a road. Turn left, ignore the first public footpath sign on the right but at the second one, turn right along a tarmac drive (**Mill Lane**).

Follow this winding tree-lined drive through a valley – there is a stream on the left – passing to the left of the former mill buildings and crossing a bridge over the infant **river Weaver**. Continue along the drive to where it bends right, keep ahead to climb a stile and walk along the left edge of a field. Climb a stile, cross a track, climb another stile opposite and follow the direction of the arrow across the next field, making for the right edge where you go through a gate onto a track. Walk along the hedge-lined track and just before a canal bridge, turn right through a gate and descend steps to the towpath of the **Shropshire Union Canal**.

The Shropshire Union Canal was built by Thomas Telford and opened in 1835. It runs for approximately 66 miles from the edge of Wolverhampton to the river Mersey at Ellesmere Port. At Audlem it climbs over 90 ft from the Cheshire Plain by means of a flight of 15 locks.

 ③

Turn sharp left to pass under the bridge and follow the towpath back to **Audlem**. At the **Shroppie Fly**, switch to the vehicle track parallel to the towpath, passing **Audlem Mill** (now a canal shop and workshop) to the road. Turn left through the village to return to the start.

The church and market cross at Audlem

PLACE OF INTEREST NEARBY

The **Secret Nuclear Bunker** at Hack Green is a unique visitor attraction. It brings back memories of the post-war years of the Cold War as you go through the massive doors and are transported underground into the secret bunker. Telephone: 01270 629219.

20 | Around Malpas

Distance 3 miles **Terrain** Lanes and undulating field paths
Map OS Explorer 257 Crewe & Nantwich (GR 487473)

How to get there

Malpas lies 6 miles to the north-west of Whitchurch. From the A41 Chester to Whitchurch road, take either the B5395 or B5069. **Parking:** Free car parks at Malpas.

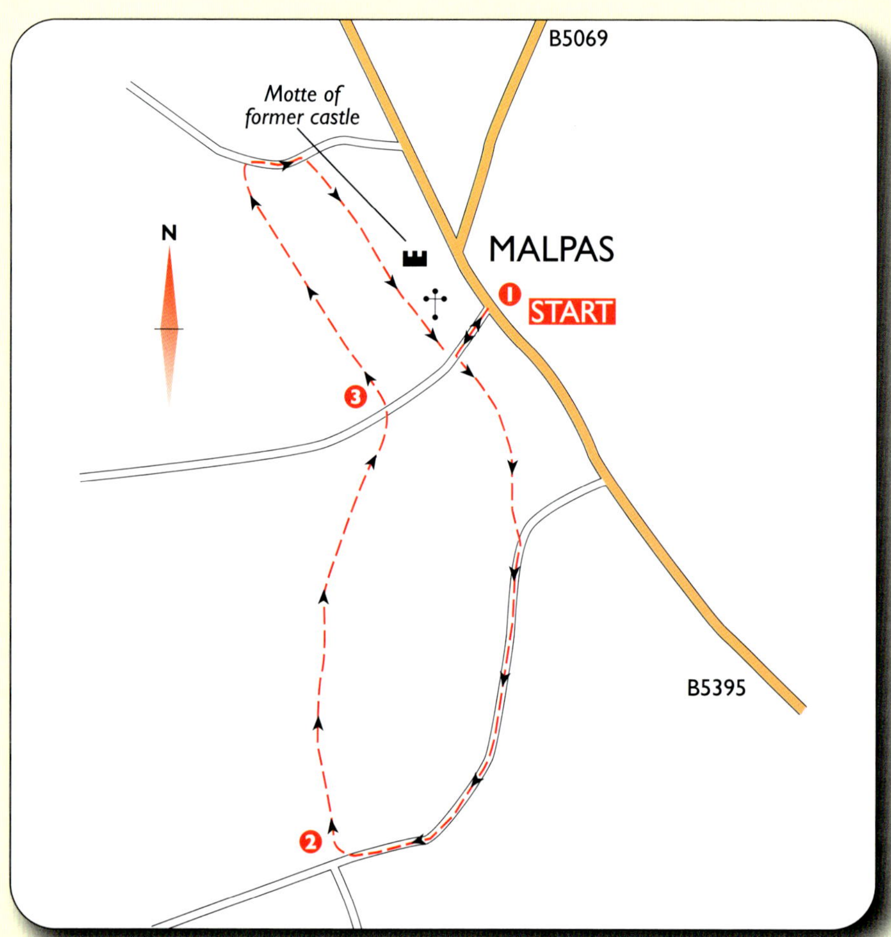

Introduction

The walk explores the attractive countryside immediately to the west of Malpas, with a number of fine views looking westwards towards Wales. A gentle descent across a field is followed by a short stroll along a quiet lane. Then comes an equally gentle and easy climb across fields to the edge of the village from where a quick return to the start can easily be made. But the short additional stroll is definitely to be recommended as it is on this stretch, which takes in the highest points on the walk, that you enjoy the finest views. Towards the end you pass both the motte of the former castle and the superb medieval church.

Refreshments

Malpas has several pubs and cafés. An unusual and very pleasant environment in which to enjoy a light lunch is the **Coffee Station**, housed in the village's former fire station. As well as a wide choice of lunches (sandwiches, paninis, omelettes, jacket potatoes and soups), the café also serves breakfast, morning coffee, afternoon tea and cakes. Telephone: 01948 860989.

THE WALK

The attractive old village of Malpas lies huddled around its hilltop church and castle mound close to the border with Wales. Dominating the village is the impressive sandstone church, built in the late 14th century and extensively altered in the 15th century. Just to the north is the 11th-century motte or mound, visible from the churchyard. The Market Cross at the bottom of Church Street, the starting point of the walk, is a Victorian replacement of an earlier one.

Begin by the **Market Cross** at the bottom of **Church Street** and walk up the street. Opposite the church, turn left along a track (**Parbutts Lane**), go through a kissing gate and head gently downhill along the left edge of a field. At a junction of paths – there is a kissing gate here on the left – bear right, continue downhill across the field and in the bottom corner go through a kissing gate onto a lane. Walk along the lane and follow it around a right bend.

Just beyond a junction with another lane, turn right through a kissing gate, at a public footpath sign to **Malpas**. Head across a field, keeping parallel to a fence on the left, to a kissing gate, go through and continue across the next field to a gate. Go through, keep along the right edge of the next two fields and in the far corner of the second field, turn right through a gate. After descending a slope, go through a kissing gate, walk diagonally across a field and go through another kissing gate in the corner. Bear slightly left and keep in a straight line across the next field towards the houses of **Malpas**, making for a footbridge on the far side. Cross it, bear slightly left again, head gently uphill across a field and on the far side, turn right to continue along its top edge. At a hedge corner, look out for where you turn left through a kissing gate and walk along a hedge-lined path to emerge onto a road on the edge of **Malpas**.

Drive and Stroll

3 Turn right, take the first road on the left and at a public footpath sign about 20 yards ahead, bear right onto an enclosed path, passing to the right of houses to reach a kissing gate. Go through to enter a field and at a junction of paths, keep ahead to join and keep alongside the right field edge to a kissing gate. Go through, continue along a left field edge, marked by a line of fine old trees, go through another kissing gate, head gently down across the next field and a kissing gate and steps bring you onto a lane. Turn right, head gently uphill along this narrow sunken lane and, at a public footpath sign, turn right up steps and go through a gate. Walk across a field, veering left and making for a kissing gate on the far side. Go through and keep ahead along an enclosed path. Cross a tarmac track and continue along the enclosed path which emerges in **Malpas churchyard**. Keep ahead, passing the motte on the left and, in front of the church turn right to a road. Turn left; at a T-junction turn left again into **Church Street** and retrace your steps downhill to return to the start.

PLACE OF INTEREST NEARBY

Cholmondeley Castle Gardens lie just off the A49, about 5 miles north of Whitchurch. These extensive landscaped gardens include a children's play area, picnic site and tearoom. Telephone: 01829 720383.